LAILI AND MAJNUN

LAILI AND MAJNUN;

A POEM.

FROM THE ORIGINAL PERSIAN OF NAZAMI.

BY

JAMES ATKINSON, ESQ.

GYAN

Published by

GYAN

Gyan Publishing House
5, Ansari Road
Daryaganj, New Delhi-110002
Phone: 011-47034999, 9811692060
E-mail: books@gyanbooks.com

Distribution Network
gyanbooks.com
India, USA, Canada, UK, Australia, France

ISBN: 978-81-212-8224-6 (PB)
First Published, 1836

2nd Impression 2023

Printed at: Gyan Press, Delhi.

LAILI AND MAJNUN
Author: JAMES ATKINSON

LAILÍ AND MAJNUN

LAILÍ AND MAJNUN;

A POEM.

FROM THE ORIGINAL PERSIAN OF NAZAMI.

BY

JAMES ATKINSON, ESQ.

OF THE HONORABLE EAST INDIA COMPANY'S BENGAL MEDICAL SERVICE:

AUTHOR OF

SOHRAB, A POEM; AN ABRIDGMENT IN PROSE AND VERSE OF THE SHAH-NAMEH OF FIRDAUSI; LA SECCHIA RAPITA, FROM THE ITALIAN OF TASSONI, &c. &c.

The course of true love never did run smooth.

Lovers and madmen have such seething brains,
Such shaping fantasies that apprehend,
More than cool reason comprehends.

He will not be commanded.

SHAKSPEARE.

PUBLISHED UNDER THE SUPERINTENDENCE OF THE ORIENTAL TRANSLATION FUND OF GREAT BRITAIN AND IRELAND.

LONDON:

A. J. VALPY, M.A.

PUBLISHER TO THE ORIENTAL TRANSLATION FUND, &c.

RED LION COURT, FLEET STREET.

M.DCCC.XXXVI.

PREFACE.

THE story of the loves of Lailí and Majnún is one of the most popular in the East. There are several poems on the same subject by different authors, but that by Nazámi is considered the best; and I believe this is the first time it has appeared in the European language.

Every nation has its favourite tales of love as well as chivalry. France and Italy have their Abelard and Eloisa, their Petrarch and Laura; and Arabia has its Lailí and Majnún, the beautiful record of whose sorrows is constantly referred to, throughout the East, as an immortal example of the most faithful love. The reader will, I think, be pleased with the manner in which the Persian poet has depicted the character of a frantic lover, and also the tender affections of his Lailí. The sentiments will be found to differ very little from those of the Western world. Human nature is every where the same.

Nazámi is said to be a native of Ganja, or Kenja, near Tefflis, and flourished in the twelfth century, or sixth of the Mohammedan era. He died about the 597th year of the Hijrah; but no mention is made where he was buried.

Besides Lailí and Majnún, he wrote the story of Khosrú and Shirín, the Treasury of Secrets, and some other works. His last and most considerable poem was the Sekandar-Namea, an epic, celebrating the career of Alexander the Great. At the period it was finished, he is reported to have been more than sixty years of age.

Nazámi was eminently distinguished through life for his rigid sanctity, which formed indeed the peculiarity of his character, cherishing, as he did at the same time, the amatory or metaphysical sentiments which pervade his romantic poem of Lailí and Majnún. But he may have been a Súfi, and aimed at describing the passions of the soul in its progress to eternity. The Odes of Hafiz have been supposed to have a similar spiritual object!

In honour of Nazámi, it is related that Ata Beg was desirous of forming and cultivating an acquaintance with him, and with that view ordered one of his courtiers to request his attendance. But it was replied, that Nazámi, being an austere recluse, studiously avoided all intercourse with princes. Ata Beg, on hearing this, and suspecting that the extreme piety and abstinence of Nazámi were affected, waited upon him in great pomp for the purpose of tempting and seducing him from his obscure retreat; but the result was highly favourable to the poet; and the prince ever afterwards looked upon him as a truly holy man, frequently visiting him, and treating him with the most profound respect and veneration. Nazámi also received many substantial proofs of the admiration in which his genius and learning were held. On one occasion, five thousand dinars were sent to him, and on another he was presented with an estate consisting of fourteen villages. The brief notice in Dowlat Shah's account of the Poets of Persia represents him as the finest writer of the age in which he lived. Hafiz thus speaks of him :—

> Not all the treasured store of ancient days
> Can boast the sweetness of Nazámi's lays.

Barrackpore,
December 20th, 1835.

LAILÍ AND MAJNÚN.

I.

SAKI, thou know'st I worship wine;
Let that delicious cup be mine.
Wine! pure and limpid as my tears,
Dispeller of a lover's fears;
With thee inspired, with thee made bold,
'Midst combat fierce my post I hold;
With thee inspired, I touch the string,
And, rapt, of love and pleasure sing.
Thou art a lion, seeking prey,
Along the glades where wild deer stray;
And like a lion I would roam,
To bring the joys I seek for home;
With wine, life's dearest, sweetest treasure,
I feel the thrill of every pleasure:
—Bring, Saki, bring the ruby now;
Its lustre sparkles on thy brow,

And, flashing with a tremulous light,
Has made thy laughing eyes more bright:
Bring, bring the liquid gem, and see
Its power, its wond'rous power, in me.
—No ancestors have I to boast;
The trace of my descent is lost.
From Adam what do I inherit?
What but a sad and troubled spirit?
For human life, from oldest time,
Is ever mark'd with guilt and crime;
And man, betrayer and betray'd,
Lurks like a spider in the shade;
But wine still plays a magic part,
Exalting high the drooping heart.
Then, Saki, linger not, but give
The blissful balm on which I live.
Come, bring the juice of the purple vine,
Bring, bring the musky-scented wine;
A draught of wine the memory clears,
And wakens thoughts of other years.—
When blushing dawn illumes the sky,
Fill up a bumper, fill it high!
That wine, which to the fever'd lip,
With anguish parch'd, when given to sip,
Imparts a rapturous smile, and throws
A veil o'er all distracting woes:
That wine, the lamp which, night and day,
Lights us along our weary way;

Which strews the path with fruits and flowers,
And gilds with joy our fleeting hours;
And lifts the mind, now grown elate,
To Jamshid's glory, Jamshid's state.—
But of the kingly race beware;
'Tis not for thee their smiles to share:
Smiles are deceitful, fire looks bright,
And sheds a lucid dazzling light;
But, though attractive, it is known
That safety dwells in flight alone.
The moth the taper's radiance tries,
But 'midst the flame in torment dies:
And none lament that foolish pride
Which seeks to be with kings allied.—
Bring, bring the musky-scented wine!
'Tis the key of mirth, and must be mine:
The key which opens wide the door
Of rapture's rich and varied store;
Which makes the mounting spirits glad,
And feel the pomp of Kai-Kobâd.
Wine o'er the temper casts a spell
Of kindness indescribable:
Then, since I'm in the drinking vein,
Bring, bring the luscious wine again!
From the vintner another fresh supply.
And let not the reveller's lips be dry.—
Come, Saki, thou'rt not old, nor lame;
Thou'dst not incur from a minstrel blame;

Let him wash from his heart the dust of sorrow;
Let him riot in social bliss till the morrow;
Let the sound of the goblet delight his ear,
Like the music that breathes from Heaven's own sphere.

II.

Mark, where instruction pours upon the mind
The light of knowledge, simple or refined;
Shaikhs of each tribe have children there, and each
Studies whate'er the bearded sage can teach.
Thence his attainments Kais assiduous drew,
And scattered pearls from lips of ruby hue;
And there, of different tribe and gentle mien,
A lovely maid of tender years was seen:
Her mental powers an early bloom displayed:
Her peaceful form in simple garb array'd
Bright as the morn, her cypress shape, and eyes
Dark as the stag's, were view'd with fond surprise:
And when her cheek this Arab moon reveal'd,
A thousand hearts were won; no pride, no shield,
Could check her beauty's power, resistless grown,
Given to enthral and charm—but chiefly one.
Her richly flowing locks were black as night,
And Lailí she was call'd—that heart's delight:
One single glance the nerves to frenzy wrought,
One single glance bewilder'd every thought;
And, when o'er Kais affection's blushing rose
Diffused its sweetness, from him fled repose:

Tumultuous passion danced upon his brow;
He sought to woo her, but he knew not how:
He gazed upon her cheek, and, as he gazed,
Love's flaming taper more intensely blazed.
Soon mutual pleasure warm'd each other's heart;
Love conquer'd both—they never dreamt to part;
And, while the rest were poring o'er their books,
They pensive mused, and read each other's looks:
While other schoolmates for distinction strove,
And thought of fame, they only thought of love:
While others various climes in books explored,
Both idly sat—adorer and adored:
Science for them had now no charms to boast;
Learning for them had all its virtue lost:
Their only taste was love, and love's sweet ties,
And writing ghazels to each other's eyes.

Yes, love triumphant came, engrossing all
The fond luxuriant thoughts of youth and maid;
And, whilst subdued in that delicious thrall,
Smiles and bright tears upon their features play'd.
Then in soft converse did they pass the hours,—
Their passion, like the season, fresh and fair;
Their opening path seem'd deck'd with balmiest flowers,
Their melting words as soft as summer air.

Immersed in love so deep,
They hoped suspicion would be lull'd asleep,

And none be conscious of their amorous state;
They hoped that none with prying eye,
And gossip tongue invidiously,
Might to the busy world its truth relate:
And, thus possess'd, they anxious thought
Their passion would be kept unknown;
Wishing to seem what they were not,
Though all observed their hearts were one.

By worldly prudence uncontroll'd,
Their every glance their feelings told;
For true love never yet had skill
To veil impassion'd looks at will.
When ringlets of a thousand curls,
And ruby lips, and teeth of pearls,
And dark eyes flashing quick and bright,
Like lightning on the brow of night—
When charms like these their power display,
And steal the wilder'd heart away—
Can man, dissembling, coldly seem
Unmoved as by an idle dream?
Kais saw her beauty, saw her grace,
The soft expression of her face;
And as he gazed, and gazed again,
Distraction stung his burning brain:
No rest he found by day or night—
Lailí for ever in his sight.

But, oh! when separation came,
More brightly glow'd his ardent flame;
And she, with equal sorrow fraught,
Bewail'd the fate upon them brought.
—He wander'd wild through lane and street,
With frantic step, as if to meet
Something which still his search defied,
Reckless of all that might betide.
His bosom heaved with groans and sighs,
Tears ever gushing from his eyes;
And still he struggled to conceal
The anguish he was doom'd to feel;
And, maddened with excessive grief,
In the lone desert sought relief.
Thither, as morning dawn'd, he flew;
His head and feet no covering knew;
And every night, with growing pain,
The woes of absence mark'd his strain.
The secret path he eager chose
Where Laili's distant mansion rose;
And kiss'd the door, and in that kiss
Fancied he quaff'd the cup of bliss.
How fleet his steps to that sweet place!
A thousand wings increased his pace;
But thence, his fond devotions paid,
A thousand thorns his course delay'd.

III.

The lover from his mistress parted,
Lingering, oppress'd, and broken-hearted,
Sank, like the sun all rayless, down—
Khosrú, without his throne or crown.
With matted locks and bosom bare,
Unshielded from the scorching air,
This hapless youth, absorb'd in grief,
Hoped with his friends to find relief;
The few, by strong affection bound,
And, 'midst his woes, still faithful found.
But vain the refuge—friendship's smile
Could not his love-lorn heart beguile:
Again he hasten'd to that place remote,
  Where all he loved in life had gone:
He call'd her magic name, but she was not,
  Nor of her kindred, one, not one,
In that sequester'd lonely spot:
He call'd a thousand times, but call'd in vain;
None heeded, for none heard the strain;
And thence no fond reply that hapless youth could gain.

Lailí had, with her kindred, been removed
  Among the Nijid mountains, where
She cherish'd still the thoughts of him she loved,
And her affection thus more deeply proved
  Amid that wild retreat. Kais sought her there;

Sought her in rosy bower and silent glade,
Where the tall palm-trees flung refreshing shade.
He call'd upon her name again;
Again he call'd, alas! in vain;
His voice unheard, though raised on every side;
Echo alone to his lament replied;
And Lailí! Lailí! rang around,
As if enamour'd of that magic sound.
Dejected and forlorn, fast-falling dew
Glisten'd upon his cheeks of pallid hue;
Through grove and frowning glen he lonely stray'd,
And with his griefs the rocks were vocal made.
Beautiful Lailí! had she gone for ever?—
Could he that thought support? oh, never, never!
Whilst deep emotion agonised his breast,
He to the morning-breeze these words address'd:—

"Breeze of the morn! so fresh and sweet,
Wilt thou my blooming mistress greet;
And, nestling in her glossy hair,
My tenderest thoughts, my love, declare?
Wilt thou, while 'mid her tresses sporting,
Their odorous balm, their perfume courting,
Say to that soul-seducing maid,
In grief how prostrate I am laid!
And gently whisper in her ear
This message, with an accent clear:—

'Thy form is ever in my sight,
In thought by day, in dreams by night;
For one, in spirits sad and broken,
That mole would be the happiest token;
That mole which adds to every look
A magic spell I cannot brook;
For he who sees thy melting charms,
And does not feel his soul in arms,
Bursting with passion, rapture, all
That speak love's deepest, wildest thrall,
Must be, as Káf's ice-summit, cold,
And, haply, scarce of human mould.
Let him, unmoved by charms like thine,
His worthless life at once resign—
Those lips are sugar, heavenly sweet;
O let but mine their pouting meet!
The balsam of delight they shed;
Their radiant colour ruby-red.
The Evil eye has struck my heart,
But thine in beauty sped the dart:
Thus many a flower, of richest hue,
Hath fall'n and perish'd where it grew;
Thy beauty is the sun in brightness,
Thy form a Peri's self in lightness;
A treasure thou, which, poets say,
The heavens would gladly steal away—
Too good, too pure, on earth to stay!' "

IV.

As morning broke, the sun, with golden light,
Eclipsed the twinkling stars of silvery white;
And Majnún, rising, eagerly pursued
The path which wound to Lailí's solitude,
Grieved to the heart; and, as he went along,
His lips breathed softly some impassion'd song;
Some favorite lay, which tenderly express'd
The present feeling of his anxious breast.
In fancy soon her image he beheld;
No shadowy cloud her lucid beauty veil'd;
He saw her fresh as morning's scented air—
Himself exhausted by incessant care:
He saw her blooming as the blushing rose—
Himself dejected by unnumber'd woes:
He saw her like an angel soft and bland—
Himself consuming like a lighted brand:
Her ringlets flowing loosely to the ground,
His ringlets, fetters by affection bound;
And still, all faint with grief, he pass'd his days,
Pouring his soul out in melodious lays.

His friends, to whom his griefs are known.
His altered aspect now bemoan;
Alarm'd to hear the sufferer still
In frantic mood unceasing fill

The night-breeze with his plaintive woes;
For sorrow with indulgence grows.
They try to soothe his wilder'd mind,
Where reason once was seen enshrined;
His father, with a father's love,
Sought his sad sorrows to remove,
And gave him maxims full and clear,
And counsel meet for youth to hear.
But, though good counsel and advice
May often lead to Paradise,
When love has once the heart engross'd,
All counsel, all advice is lost;
And weeping Majnún not a word
Of his poor father's counsel heard,
Ah! when did prudence e'er control
The frenzy of a love-lorn soul?

Disconsolate the father now
  Behind the Harem-screen appears,
Inquiring of his females how
  He best might dry the maniac's tears;
And what had drawn the sparkling moon
Of intellect from him so soon.
The answer of the old and young
Was ready, quivering on the tongue—
"His fate is fix'd—his eyes have seen
The charms of his affection's queen

In all their winning power display'd;
His heart a captive to that Arab maid.
Then what relief canst thou supply?
What to the bleeding lover, doom'd to die?
What but fulfilling his desires?
And this a father's generous aid requires.
See them united in the bands of love;
And that alone his frenzy will remove."

These words (for woman's words convey
A spell, converting night to day,
Diffuse o'er troubled life a balm,
And passion's fiercest fever calm)—
These words relieve the father's heart,
And comfort to his thoughts impart.
Resolved at once, he now with speed
Marshals his followers, man and steed;
And, all assembled, bends his way
To the damsel's home, without delay.

Approaching, quick the enquiry rose—
—"Come ye hither as friends or foes?
Whatever may your errand be.
That errand must be told to me;
For none, unless a sanction'd friend,
Can pass the boundary I defend."

This challenge touch'd Syd Omri's pride:
And yet he calmly thus replied,—
"I come in friendship, and propose
All future chance of feud to close."
Then to the maiden's father said,—
"The nuptial feast may now be spread:
My son with thirsty heart has seen
Thy fountain pure with margin green;
And every fountain, clear and bright,
Gives to the thirsty heart delight.
That fountain he demands. With shame,
Possess'd of power, and wealth, and fame,
I to his silly humour bend,
And humbly seek his fate to blend
With one inferior. Need I tell
My own high lineage, known so well?
If sympathy my heart incline,
Or vengeance, still the means are mine.
Treasure and arms can amply bear
Me through the toils of desert-war;
But thou'rt the merchant, pedlar-chief,
And I the buyer; come, sell,—be brief!
If thou art wise, accept advice;
Sell, and receive a princely price!"

The sire of Lailí mark'd his haughty tone,
But smoothly answer'd,—"Not on us alone

Depends the nuptial union—but on Heaven,
By which all power, and right, and truth are given.
However just our reasoning may appear,
We 're still beset by endless error here;
And proffer'd friendship may perchance become
The harbinger of strife and of the tomb;
Madness is neither sin nor crime, we know,
But who'd be link'd to madness or a foe?
Thy son is mad—his senses first restore;
In constant prayer the aid of Heaven implore;
But while portentous gloom pervades his brain,
Disturb me not with this vain suit again.
The jewel, sense, no purchaser can buy,
Nor treachery the place of sense supply.
Thou hast my reasons—and this parley o'er,
Keep them in mind, and trouble me no more!"
Abash'd, his very heartstrings torn,
Thus to be met with scoff and scorn,
Syd Omri to his followers turn'd,
His cheek with kindled anger burn'd;
But, scorning more to do or say,
Indignant homeward urged his way.
  And now for a disorder'd mind,
What med'cine can affection find?
What magic power, what human skill,
To rectify the erring will?
—The necromancer's art they tried—
Charms, philtres used, to win a bride,

And make a father's heart relent,
As if by Heaven in pity sent.—
Vain efforts all. They now address
Kind words, his mind to soothe and bless,
And urge in his unwilling ear
(Treason and death for him to hear)
"Another love, of nobler race,
Unmatch'd in form, unmatch'd in grace;
All blandishments and fairy wiles;
Her every glance the heart beguiles:
An idol of transcendent worth,
With charms eclipsing royal birth;
Whose balmy lips like rubies glow;
Sugar and milk their sweetness show;
And her words like softest music flow:
Adorn'd in all the pride of spring,
Her robes around rich odours fling;
Sparkling with gold and gems, she seems
The bright perfection of a lover's dreams;
Then why, with such a prize at home,
For charms inferior amid strangers roam?
Bid all unduteous thoughts depart,
And wisely banish Lailí from thy heart."
When Majnún saw his hopes decay,
Their fairest blossoms fade away;
And friends and sire, who might have been
Kind intercessors, rush between

Him and the only wish that shed
One ray of comfort round his head,
(His fondly cherish'd Arab maid),
He beat his hands, his garments tore,
He cast his fetters on the floor
In broken fragments, and in wrath
Sought the dark wilderness's path;
And there he wept and sobb'd aloud,
Unwitness'd by the gazing crowd;
His eyes all tears, his soul all flame,
Repeating still his Lailí's name.
And Lailí! Lailí! echoed round,
Still dwelling on that rapturous sound.
—In pilgrim-garb he reckless stray'd,
No covering on his feet or head;
And still, as memory touch'd his brain,
He murmur'd some love-wilder'd strain:
But still her name was ever on his tongue,
And Lailí! Lailí! still through grove and forest rung.

Sad inmate of the desert wild,
His form and face with dust defiled;
Exhausted with his grief's excess,
He sat him down in weariness.
"Estranged from friends," he weeping cried,
"My homeward course is dark to me;
But, Lailí, were I at thy side,
How bless'd would thy poor lover be!

My kindred think of me with shame;
My friends they shudder at my name.

That cup of wine I held, alas!
Dropp'd from my hand, is dash'd in pieces;
And thus it is that, like the glass,
Life's hope in one dark moment ceases.
O ye who never felt distress,
Never gay scenes of joy forsaking,
Whose minds, at peace, no cares oppress,
What know ye of a heart that's breaking!"

* * * * *

Worn out at length, he sank upon the ground,
And there in tears the mournful youth is found
By those who traced his wanderings: gently they
Now to Syd Omri's home the faded form convey:
His sire and kinsmen round him moan,
And, weeping, make his griefs their own;
And, garrulous, recall to memory's eye
The progress of his life from infancy—
The flattering promise of his boyish days—
And find the wreck of hope on which they gaze.
They deem'd that Mecca's sacred fane
His reason would restore again;
That blessed boon to mortals given,
The arc of earth, the arc of heaven;
The holy Kába where the Prophet pray'd,
Where Zam-Zam's waters yield their saving aid.

'Tis now the season of the pilgrimage,
And now assemble merchant, chieftain, sage,
With vows and offerings, on that spot divine:
Thousands and thousands throng the splendid shrine.
And now, on that high purpose bent, await
Syd Omri's camels, ready at his gate;
Around their necks the tinkling bells are hung,
Rich tassell'd housings on their backs are flung;
And Majnún, faint, and reckless what may be,
Is on a litter placed—sad sight to see!—
And tenderly caress'd, whilst born along
By the rough moving camel, fleet and strong.
The desert soon is pass'd, and Mecca's bright
And glittering minarets rise upon the sight;
Where golden gifts, and sacrifice, and prayer,
Secure the absolution sought for there.
The father, entering that all-powerful shrine,
Thus prays—"Have mercy, Heaven, on me and mine!
O from my son this frenzied mood remove,
And save him, save him from the bane of love!"
  Majnún at this, poor wayward child,
  Look'd in his father's face and smiled;
  And frankly said his life should prove
  The truth and holiness of love.
  "My heart is bound by beauty's spell,
  My love is indestructible.
  Am I to separate from my own,
  From her for whom I breathe alone?

What friend could wish me to resign
A love so pure, so true as mine?
What, though I like a taper burn,
And almost to a shadow turn,
I envy not the heart that's free—
Love's soul-encircling chains for me!"

The love that springs from Heaven is bless'd;
Unholy passions stain the rest;
That is not love: wild fancy's birth,
Which lives on change, is constant never:
But Majnún's love was not of earth,
Glowing with heavenly truth for ever;
An earthly object raised the flame,
But 'twas from Heaven the inspiration came.

In silent sorrow the aged sire
Found all his cares were vain;
And back to his expecting tribe
Address'd his steps again;
For Mecca had no power to cool
The lover's burning brain;
No consolation, no relief
For the old man's heart-consuming grief.

V.

Sweet Lailí's kinsmen now describe
To the haughty chieftain of their tribe,

A youth amidst the desert seen,
In strange attire, of frantic mien;
His arms outstretch'd, his head all bare,
And floating loose his clustering hair:
" In a distracted mood," they say—
" He wanders hither every day;
And often, with fantastic bound,
Dances, or prostrate hugs the ground;
Or, in a voice the soul to move,
Warbles the melting songs of love;
Songs which, when breathed in tones so true,
A thousand hearts at once subdue.
He speaks—and all who listen hear
Words which they hold in memory dear;
And we and thine endure the shame,
And Lailí blushes at his name."
And now the chieftain, roused to wrath,
Threatens to cross the maniac's path.

But, haply, to prevent that barbarous deed,
  To Omri's palmy groves the tidings flew,
  And soon the father sends a chosen few
To seek the lost one. Promptly they proceed
  O'er open plain and thicket deep,
  Embowering glen and rocky steep,
  Exploring with unwearied eye
  Wherever man might pass or lie,

O'ercome by grief or death. In vain
Their sight on every side they strain,
No Majnún's voice, nor form, to cheer
Their anxious hearts ; but far and near
The yell of prowling beasts they hear.
Mournful they deem him lost or dead,
And tears of bitterest anguish shed.
But he, the wanderer from his home,
Found not from beasts a living tomb;
His passion's pure and holy flame
Their native fierceness seem'd to tame;
Tiger and ravenous wolf pass'd by him,
The fell hyena came not nigh him ;
As if, ferocious spirits to quell,
His form had been invisible,
Or bore a life-protecting spell.
Upon a fountain emerald brink
Majnún had stoop'd its lucid wave to drink;
And his despairing friends descried
Him laid along that murmuring fountain's side,
Wailing his sorrows still; his feeble voice
Dwelt, ever dwelt, upon his heart's sole choice.
A wild emotion trembled in his eye,
His bosom wrung with many a deep-drawn sigh;
And groans, and tears, and music's softest lay,
Successive mark'd his melancholy day.
—Now he is stretch'd along the burning sand,
A stone his pillow—now, upraised his hand,

He breathes a prayer for Lailí, and again
The desert echoes with some mournful strain.
As wine deprives us of the sense we boast,
So reason in love's maddening draughts is lost.

Restored to home again, he dreads to meet
His father's frowns, and bends to kiss his feet;
Then, gazing wildly, rises up, and speaks,
And in a piteous tone forgiveness seeks:—
"Sad is my fate, o'ercast my youthful morn,
My rose's leaves, my life's sweet buds are torn;
I sit in darkness, ashes o'er my head,
To all the world's alluring pleasures dead;
For me what poor excuse can soothe thy mind?
But thou 'rt my father still—O still be kind!"
Syd Omri his unchanged affection proved,
And, folding to his breast the child he loved,
Exclaim'd:—"My boy! I grieve to mark
Thy reason erring still, and dark;
A fire consuming every thread
Of which thy thrilling nerves are made.
Sit down, and from thy eyesight tear
The poisonous thorn that rankles there:
'Tis best we should to mirth incline,
But let it not be raised by wine:
'Tis well desire should fill the breast;
Not such desire as breaks our rest.

Remain not under grief's control,
Nor taunt of foe which stings the soul;
Let wisdom every movement guide;
Error but swells affliction's tide;
Though love hath set thee all on fire,
And thy heart burns with still unquench'd desire,
Despair not of a remedy;
From seedling springs the shady tree;
From hope continued follows gladness,
Which dull despair had lost in sadness;
Associate with the wealthy, they
Will show to glittering wealth the way;
A wanderer never gathers store,
Be thou a wanderer now no more.
Wealth opens every door, and gives
Command, and homage still receives:
Be patient then, and patience will
By slow degrees thy coffers fill.
That river rolling deep and broad,
Once but a narrow streamlet flow'd;
That lofty mountain, now in view,
Its height from small beginnings drew.
He who impatient hurries on,
Hoping for gems, obtains a stone;
Shrewdness and cunning gain the prize,
While wisdom's self unprosperous lies:
The fox of crafty subtle mind
Leaves the wolf's dulness far behind;

Be thou discreet, thy thoughts employ,
The world's inviting pomp enjoy.—
In search of wealth from day to day
Love's useless passion dies away;
The sensual make disease their guest,
And nourish scorpions in their breast.
And is thy heart so worthless grown,
To be the cruel sport of one?
Keep it from woman's scathe, and still
Obedient to thy own free will,
And mindful of a parent's voice,
Make him, and not thy foes, rejoice."

Majnún replied:—"My father!—father still!—
My power is gone; I cannot change my will:
The moral counsel thou hast given to me,
(To one who cannot from his bondage flee,)
Avails me nothing. 'Tis no choice of mine,
But Fate's decree, that I should thus repine:
Stand I alone? Look round, on every side
Are broken hearts, by sternest fortune tried:
Shadows are not self-made—the silver moon
Is not self-station'd, but the Almighty's boon.
From the huge elephant's stupendous form,
To that of the poor ant, the smallest worm,
Through every grade of life, all power is given,
All joy or anguish by the Lord of Heaven.

I sought not, I, misfortune—but it came—
I sought not fire, yet is my heart all flame:
They ask me why I never laugh nor smile,
Though laughter be no sign of sense the while.
If I should laugh in merry mood, a-gape,
Amidst my mirth some secret might escape.
—A partridge seized an ant, resolved to kill
The feeble creature with his horny bill;
When, laughing loud, the ant exclaimed—'Alas!
A partridge thou! and art thou such an ass?
I'm but a gnat, and dost thou think to float
A gnat's slight filmy texture down thy throat?'
The partridge laugh'd at this unusual sound,
And, laughing, dropp'd the ant upon the ground.
Thus he who idly laughs will always find
Some grief succeed—'tis so with all mankind.
The stupid partridge, laughing, droop'd his crest,
And by that folly lost what he possess'd.
—This poor old drudge, which bears its heavy load,
Must all life long endure the same rough road;
No joy for him, in mortal aid no trust,
No rest till death consigns him to the dust."

Here paused the youth, and wept; and now
The household smooth his furrow'd brow,
And with unceasing eagerness
Seek to remove his soul's distress.

But grief, corroding grief, allows no space
For quiet thoughts ; his wounds break out anew ;
His kindred every change of feature trace,
And unavailing tears their cheeks bedew ;
A deeper, keener anguish marks his face ;
His faded form so haggard to the view ;
Useless the task his sorrows to remove,
For who can free the heart from love, unchanging love ?

Few days had pass'd, when, frantic grown,
He burst from his domestic prison,
And in the desert wild, alone,
Pour'd, like the morning bird, new risen,
His ardent lay of love. Not long
The mountains echoed with his song,
Ere, drawn by sounds so sweet and clear,
A crowd of listeners hover'd near :
They saw him, tall as cypress, stand,
A rocky fragment in his hand ;
A purple sash his waist around,
His legs with links of iron bound ;
Yet, unencumber'd was his gait ;
They only show'd his maniac state.

* * * * *

Wandering he reach'd a spot of ground,
With palmy groves and poplars crown'd ;
A lively scene it was to view,
Where flowers too bloom'd of every hue ;

Starting, he saw the axe applied
To a cypress-tree—and thus he cried:—
"Gardener! did ever love thy heart control?
Was ever woman mistress of thy soul?
When joy has thrill'd through every glowing nerve,
Hadst thou no wish that feeling to preserve?
Does not a woman's love delight, entrance,
And every blessing fortune yields enhance?
Then stop that lifted hand, the stroke suspend,
Spare, spare the cypress-tree, and be my friend!
And why? Look there, and be forewarn'd by me,
'Tis Lailí's form, all grace and majesty;
Wouldst thou root up resemblance so complete,
And lay its branches withering at thy feet?
What! Lailí's form? no; spare the cypress-tree;
Let it remain, still beautiful and free;
Yes, let my prayers thy kindliest feelings move,
And save the graceful shape of her I love!"
—The gardener dropp'd his axe, o'ercome with shame,
And left the tree to bloom, and speak of Lailí's fame.

VI.

Lailí in beauty, softness, grace,
Surpass'd the loveliest of her race;
She was a fresh and odorous flower,
Pluck'd by a fairy from her bower;
With heart-delighting rosebuds blooming,
The welcome breeze of spring perfuming.

The killing witchery that lies
In her soft, black, delicious eyes,
When gather'd in one amorous glance,
Pierces the heart, like sword or lance;
The prey that falls into her snare,
For life must mourn and struggle there:
Her eyelash speaks a thousand blisses,
Her lips of ruby ask for kisses;
Soft lips where sugar-sweetness dwells,
Sweet as the bee-hive's honey-cells;
Her cheeks, so beautiful and bright,
Had stole the moon's refulgent light;
Her form the cypress-tree expresses,
And full and ripe invites caresses;
With all these charms the heart to win,
There was a careless grief within—
Yet none beheld her grief, or heard;
She droop'd like broken-winged bird.
Her secret thoughts her love concealing,
But, softly to the terrace stealing,
From morn to eve she gazed around,
In hopes her Majnún might be found,
Wandering in sight. For she had none
To sympathise with her—not one!
None to compassionate her woes—
In dread of rivals, friends, and foes;
And though she smiled, her mind's distress
Fill'd all her thoughts with bitterness:

The fire of absence on them prey'd,
But light nor smoke that fire betray'd;
Shut up within herself, she sate,
Absorb'd in grief, disconsolate;
Yet true love has resources still,
Its soothing arts, and ever will!

Voices in guarded softness rose
  Upon her ever-listening ear;
She heard her constant lover's woes,
  In melting strains, repeated near;

The sky, with gloomy clouds o'erspread,
At length soft showers began to shed;
And what, before, destruction seem'd,
With rays of better promise gleam'd.

Voices of young and old she heard
  Beneath the harem-walls reciting
Her Majnún's songs; each thrilling word
  Her almost broken heart delighting.

Lailí, with matchless charms of face,
Was bless'd with equal mental grace;
With eloquence and taste refined;
And from the treasures of her mind
She pour'd her fondest love's confession
With faithful love's most warm expression;

Told all her hopes and sorrows o'er,
Though told a thousand times before:
The life-blood circling through her veins
Recorded her affecting strains;
And as she wrote, with passion flush'd,
The glowing words with crimson blush'd.
And now the terrace she ascends
In secret, o'er the rampart bends,
And flings the record, with a sigh,
To one that moment passing by:
Unmark'd the stranger gains the prize,
And from the spot like lightning flies
To where the lingering lover weeps unseen.
—Starting upon his feet, with cheerful mien,
He gazes, reads, devours the pleasing tale,
And joy again illumes his features pale.

Thus was resumed the soft exchange of thought;
Thus the return of tenderest feeling wrought:
Each the same secret intercourse pursued,
And mutual vows more ardently renew'd;
And many a time between them went and came
The fondest tokens of their deathless flame;
Now in hope's heaven, now in despair's abyss,
And now enrapt in visionary bliss.

VII.

The gloomy veil of night withdrawn,
How sweetly looks the silvery dawn:
Rich blossoms laugh on every tree,
Like men of fortunate destiny,
Or the shining face of revelry.
The crimson tulip and golden rose
Their sweets to all the world disclose.
I mark the glittering pearly wave
The fountain's banks of emerald lave;
The birds in every arbor sing,
The very raven hails the spring;
The partridge and the ring-dove raise
Their joyous notes in songs of praise;
But bulbuls, through the mountain-vale,
Like Majnún, chant a mournful tale.

The season of the rose has led
  Lailí to her own favorite bower;
Her cheeks the softest vermil-red,
  Her eyes the modest sumbul flower.

She has left her father's painted hall,
  She has left the terrace where she kept
Her secret watch till evening fall,
  And where she oft till midnight wept.

A golden fillet sparkling round
Her brow, her raven tresses bound;
And as she o'er the greensward tripp'd,
A train of damsels ruby-lipp'd,
Blooming like flowers of Samarkand,
Obedient bow'd to her command.
She glitter'd like a moon among
The beauties of the starry throng,
With lovely forms as Houris bright,
Or Peris glancing in the light;
And now they reach an emerald spot,
Beside a cool sequester'd grot,
And soft recline beneath the shade,
By a delicious rose-bower made:
There, in soft converse, sport, and play,
The hours unnoted glide away;
But Lailí to the Bulbul tells
What secret grief her bosom swells,
And fancies, through the rustling leaves,
She from the garden-breeze receives
The breathings of her own true love,
Fond as the cooings of the dove.

In that romantic neighbourhood
A grove of palms majestic stood;
Never in Arab desert wild
A more enchanting prospect smiled;

So fragrant, of so bright a hue,
Not Irem richer verdure knew;
Nor fountain half so clear, so sweet,
As that which flow'd at Lailí's feet.

The Grove of Palms her steps invites;
  She strolls amid its varied scenes,
  Its pleasant copses, evergreens,
In which her waken'd heart delights.
Where'er the genial zephyr sighs,
Lilies and roses near her rise:
Awhile the prospect charms her sight,
Awhile she feels her bosom light,
Her eyes with pleasure beaming bright:
But sadness o'er her spirit steals,
And thoughts, too deep to hide, reveals:
Beneath a cypress-tree reclined,
In secret thus she breathes her mind:—
"O faithful friend, and lover true,
Still distant from thy Lailí's view;
Still absent, still beyond her power
To bring thee to her fragrant bower;
O noble youth, still thou art mine,
And Lailí, Lailí still is thine!"
  As thus she almost dreaming spoke,
A voice reproachful her attention woke.

"What! hast thou banish'd prudence from thy
mind?
And shall success be given to one unkind?
Majnún on billows of despair is toss'd,
Lailí has nothing of her pleasures lost;
Majnún has sorrow gnawing at his heart,
Lailí's blithe looks far other thoughts impart;
Majnún the poison-thorn of grief endures,
Lailí, all wiles and softness, still allures;
Majnún her victim in a thousand ways,
Lailí in mirth and pastime spends her days;
Majnún's unnumber'd wounds his rest destroy,
Lailí exists but in the bowers of joy;
Majnún is bound by love's mysterious spell,
Lailí's bright cheeks of cheerful feelings tell;
Majnún his Lailí's absence ever mourns,
Lailí's light mind to other objects turns."

At this reproof tears flow'd apace
Down Lailí's pale, dejected face;
But soon to her glad heart was known
The trick, thus practised by her own
Gay, watchful, ever sportive train,
Who long had watch'd, nor watch'd in vain;
And mark'd in her love's voice and look,
Which never woman's glance mistook.
Her mother too, with keener eye,
Saw deeper through the mystery,

Which Lailí thought her story veil'd
And oft that fatal choice bewail'd;
But Lailí still loved on; the root
Sprang up, and bore both bud and fruit;
And she believed her secret flower
As safe as treasure in a guarded tower.

VIII.

That day on which she pensive stray'd
  Amidst the Grove of Palms—that day
How sweetly bloom'd the Arab maid,
  Girt by her train in fair array!
Her moist red lips, her teeth of pearl,
Her hair in many a witching curl;
Haply, on that devoted day,
A gallant youth, with followers gay,
In splendid fashion pass'd that way;
Who saw that lamp of beauty gleaming,
Her luscious eye with softness beaming;
And in his bosom rose the fire
Of still-increasing fond desire.
Resolved at once her hand to claim
(Ibn Salâm his honor'd name),
He from her parents seeks success,
  Offering the nuptial-knot to tie;
And, to promote that happiness,
  Scatters his gold abundantly,

As if it were but common earth,
Or sand, or water, little worth—
But he was of illustrious birth.
The parents scarce believed the word,
The marriage-union, thus preferr'd;
And, though consenting, still they pray'd
The nuptial morn might be delay'd:
In her no ripen'd bloom was seen,
The sweet pomegranate still was green;
But a future day should surely deck
With a bridal yoke her spotless neck;
"We will then surrender the maiden to thee.
The maiden, till now, unaffianced and free!'
The promise soothes his eager heart,
And he and his followers, pleased, depart.

IX.

Majnún, midst wild and solitude.
His melancholy mood pursued:
In sterner moments, loud he raved.
The desert's burning noon-tide braved.
Or, where refreshing shadows fell.
Warbled of her he loved so well.

The Arab chief of that domain
Which now his wandering footsteps press'd,
Was honor'd for his bounteous reign—
For ever succouring the distress'd.

Noufal his name—well known to wield,
Victorious in the battle-field,
His glittering sword, and overthrow
The robber-band or martial foe;
Magnificent in pomp and state,
And wealthy as in valour great.

One day the pleasures of the chase,
The keen pursuit of bounding deer,
Had brought the chieftain to that place
Where Majnún stood, and, drawing near,
The stranger's features sought to trace,
And the sad notes of grief to hear,
Which, ere he saw the maniac's face,
Had, sorrow-laden, struck his ear.

He now beheld that wasted frame,
That head and mien o'ergrown with hair,
That wild, wild look, which well might claim
Brotherly kindred with despair,
Dejected, miserable, borne
By grief to life's last narrow verge,
With wounded feet and vestment torn,
Singing his own funereal dirge.

Noufal had traversed forest, copse, and glade,
In anxious quest of game, and here he found

Game—but what game?—alas! a human shade,
So light it scarcely touch'd the ground.

Dismounting straight, he hears what woes
Had marr'd the mournful youth's repose;
And kindly tries with gentle words
To show what pleasures life affords;
And prove the uselessness, the folly,
Of nursing grief and melancholy;
But worse, when men from reason flee,
And willing steep their hearts in misery.

The sympathy of generous minds
Around the heart its influence winds,
And, ever soothing, by degrees,
Restores its long-lost harmonies;
Majnún, so long to love a prey,
Death hastening on by swift decay,
Began to feel that calming spell,
That sweet delight, unspeakable,
Which draws us from ourselves away.

A change now gently o'er him came;
With trembling hand he took the cup,
And drank, but drank in Lailí's name,
The life-restoring cordial up.

His spirits rose; refreshing food
  At Noufal's hospitable board
Seem'd to remove his wayward mood,
  So long endured, so long deplored.

And Noufal with delight survey'd
The social joy his eyes betray'd,
And heard his glowing strains of love,
His murmurings like the turtle-dove,
While thinking of his Arab maid.
Changed from himself, his mind at rest,
In customary robes he dress'd;
A turban shades his forehead pale,
No more is heard the lover's wail,
But, jocund as the vintner's guest,
He laughs and drinks with added zest
His dungeon gloom exchanged for day
His cheeks a rosy tint display;
He revels midst the garden's sweets,
And still his lip the goblet meets;
But so devoted, so unchanged his flame,
Never without repeating Lailí's name.

In friendly converse, heart uniting heart,
  Noufal and Majnún hand in hand are seen;
And, from each other loathing to depart,
  Wander untired by fount and meadow green.

But what is friendship to a soul
Inured to more intense control?
A zephyr breathing over flowers,
Compared to when the tempest lours?
A zephyr, friendship's gentler course;
A tempest, love's tumultuous force;
For friendship leaves a vacuum still,
Which love, and love alone, can fill:
So Majnún felt; and Noufal tried,
In vain, to fill that aching void:
For, though the liquid sparkling red
Still flow'd, his friend thus sorrowing said:—
"My generous host, with plenty bless'd,
No boding cares thy thoughts molest;
Thy kindness many a charm hath given,
But not one solace under heaven;
Without my love, in tears I languish,
And not a voice to check my anguish;
Like one of thirst about to die,
And every fountain near him dry:
Thirst is by water quench'd, not treasure,
Nor floods of wine, nor festive pleasure.
Bring me the cure my wounds require;
Quench in my heart this raging fire;
My Lailí, oh! my Lailí give,
Or thy poor friend must cease to live!"
  Majnún had scarce his wish express'd
  Ere rose in generous Noufal's breast

The firm resolve to serve his friend,
And to his settled purpose bend
Lailí's stern father;
Now, in arms array'd,
And lifting high his keen Damascus blade,
He calls a band of veterans to his aid.
Swift as the feather'd race the assembled train
Rush, sword in hand, along the desert plain;
And when the chieftain's habitation bright
Upon the blue horizon strikes the sight,
He sends a messenger to claim the bride,
In terms imperious, not to be denied;
Yet was that claim derided. "Thou wilt soon
Repent this folly:—Lailí is the moon;
And who presumes the splendid moon to gain?
Is there on earth a man so mad, so vain?
Who draw their swords at such a hazard? None.
Who strikes his crystal vase upon a stone?"
Noufal again endeavours to inspire
With dread of vengeance Lailí's haughty sire;
But useless are the threats—the same reply—
"Alike thy power and vengeance I defy!"
The parley over, Noufal draws his sword,
And with his horsemen pours upon the horde,
Ready for battle. Spears and helmets ring,
And brass-bound shields; loud twangs the archer's
string;

The field of conflict like the ocean roars,
When the huge billows burst upon the shores.
Arrows, like birds, on either foeman stood,
Drinking with open beak the vital flood;
The shining daggers in the battle's heat
Roll'd many a head beneath the horses' feet;
And lightnings, hurl'd by death's unsparing hand,
Spread consternation through the weeping land.
Amidst the horrors of that fatal fight,
Majnún appear'd—a strange appalling sight!
Wildly he raved, confounding friend and foe,
His garments half abandon'd in his woe,
And with a maniac stare reproachful cried—
"Why combat thus when all are on my side?"
The foemen laugh'd—the uproar louder grew—
No pause the brazen drums or trumpets knew;
The stoutest heart sank at the carnage wrought;
Swords blush'd to see the numerous heads they smote.
—Noufal with dragon-fierceness prowl'd around,
And hurl'd full many a warrior to the ground:
Whatever hero felt his ponderous gerz
Was crush'd, tho' stedfast as the Mount Elbêrz.
Upon whatever head his weapon fell,
There was but one heart-rending tale to tell.
Like a mad elephant the foe he met;
With hostile blood his blade continued wet;

—Wearied at length, both tribes at once withdrew,
Resolved with morn the combat to renew;
But Noufal's gallant friends had suffer'd most;
In one hour more the battle had been lost;
And thence assistance, ere the following dawn,
From other warlike tribes was promptly drawn.

The desert rang again. In front and rear
Glitter'd bright sword and buckler, gerz and spear;
Again the struggle woke the echoes round,
Swords clash'd, and blood again made red the ground;
The book of life, with dust and carnage stain'd,
Was soon destroy'd, and not a leaf remain'd.
At last, the tribe of Lailí's sire gave way,
And Noufal won the hard-contested day;
Numbers lay bleeding of that conquer'd band,
And died unsuccour'd on the burning sand.

And now the elders of that tribe appear,
Imploring the proud victor. "Chieftain, hear!
The work of slaughter is complete;
Thou seest our power destroy'd; allow
Us, wretched suppliants, at thy feet,
Humbly to ask for mercy now.

"How many warriors press the plain,
Khanjer and spear have laid them low;
At peace, behold our kinsmen slain,
And thou art now without a foe.

"Then pardon what of wrong has been:
Let us retire, unharm'd—unstay'd—
Far from this sanguinary scene,
And take thy prize—the Arab Maid."

Then came the father, full of grief, and said—
(Ashes and dust upon his hoary head,)
"With thee, alas! how useless to contend!
Thou art the conqueror, and to thee I bend.
Without resentment now the vanquish'd view,
Wounded and old, and broken-hearted too;
Reproach has fallen upon me, and has dared
To call me Persian—that I disregard;
For I'm an Arab still, and scorn the sneer
Of braggart fools, unused to shield and spear.
But let that pass. I now, o'ercome, and weak,
And prostrate, pardon from the victor seek:
Thy slave am I, obedient to thy will,
Ready thy sternest purpose to fulfil;
But if with Lailí I consent to part,
Wilt thou blot out all vengeance from thy heart?
Then speak at once, and thy behest declare:
I will not flinch, though it my soul may tear.

My daughter shall be brought at thy command;
Let the red flames ascend from blazing brand,
Waiting their victim, crackling in the air,
And Lailí duteously shall perish there.
Or, if thou 'dst rather see the maiden bleed,
This thirsty sword shall do the dreadful deed:
Dissever at one blow that lovely head,
Her sinless blood by her own father shed!
In all things thou shall find me faithful, true,
Thy slave obsequious,—what wouldst have me do?
But mark me; I am not to be beguiled;
I will not to a demon give my child;
I will not to a madman's wild embrace
Consign the pride and honor of my race,
And wed her to contempt and foul disgrace.
I will not sacrifice my tribe's fair fame,
Nor taint with obloquy her virtuous name.
Has honor on an Arab heart no claim?
Better be overwhelm'd by adverse fate
Than yield up honor, even for kingly state.
Through all Arabia is her virtue known;
Her beauty match'd by heavenly charms alone.
I'd rather in a monster be enshrined
Than bear a name detested by mankind.
What! wed a wretch, and earn my country's ban!
A dog were better than a demon-man.
A dog's bite heals, but human gnawings never;
The festering poison-wounds remain for ever."

Thus spake the father, and in Noufal's breast
Excited feelings not to be repress'd:
"I hoped to win consent," he said—
"But now that anxious hope is dead,
And thou and thine may quit the field,
Still arm'd with khanjer, sword, and shield;
Horseman and elder. Thus in vain
Blood has bedew'd this thirsty plain."

When Majnún this conclusion hears,
He flies incensed to Noufal, and with tears
Wildly exclaims—"The dawn, my generous friend!
Promised this day in happiness would end;
But thou hast let the gazelle slip away,
And me defrauded of my beauteous prey.
Near where Forát's bright stream rolls on, reclined,
Staunching my wounds, hope soothed my tortured mind,
And gave me Lailí; now that hope is cross'd,
And life's most valued charm for ever lost."

Noufal with heavy heart now homeward bent
His way, and Majnún with him sorrowing went;
And there again the pitying chieftain strove
To calm the withering pangs of hopeless love;
To bless, with gentleness and tender care,
The wounded spirit sinking in despair:

But vain his efforts; mountain, wood, and plain,
Soon heard the maniac's piercing woes again;
Escaped from listening ear, and watchful eye,
Lonely again in desert wild to lie.

X.

The minstrel strikes his soft guitar,
  With sad forebodings pale;
And fills with song the balmy air,
  And thus resumes his tale:—

  The pensive bird, compell'd to cower,
From day to day in Noufal's bower,
Tired of the scene, with pinions light,
Swift as the wind has urged its flight,
And, far from Noufal's wide domain,
Enjoys its liberty again;
Pouring aloud its sad complaint
In wildest mood without restraint.

  And now remote from peopled town,
Midst tangled forest, parch'd and brown,
The maniac roams; with double speed
He goads along his snorting steed,
Till, in a grove, a sportsman's snare
Attracts his view, and, struggling there,

Its knotted meshes fast between,
Some newly-prison'd deer are seen;
And as the sportsman forward springs
To seize on one, and promptly brings
The fatal knife upon its neck,
His hand receives a sudden check;
And looking upwards, with surprise,
(A mounted chief before his eyes!)
He stops—while thus exclaims the youth:—
"If e'er thy bosom throbb'd with ruth,
Forbear! for 'tis a crime to spill
A gazelle's blood—it bodeth ill;
Then set the pleading captive free;
For sweet is life and liberty.
That heart must be as marble hard,
And merciless as wolf or pard,
Which clouds in death that large black eye,
Beaming like Lailí's, lovingly.
The cruel stroke, my friend, withhold;
Its neck deserves a string of gold.
Observe its slender limbs, the grace
And winning meekness of its face.
The musk-pod is its fatal dower,
Like beauty, still the prey of power;
And for that fragrant gift thou 'rt led
The gentle gazelle's blood to shed!
O, seek not gain by cruel deed,
Nor let the innocent victim bleed."

"But," cried the sportsman, "these are mine;
I cannot at my task repine:
'Tis the sportsman's task, and free from blame,
To watch and snare the forest-game."

Majnún, upon this stern reply,
  Alighted from his steed, and said—
"O, let them live! they must not die.
  Forbear! and take this barb instead."
The sportsman seized it eagerly,
  And, laughing, from the greenwood sped.

Majnún, delighted, view'd his purchased prize,
And in the gazelle's sees his Lailí's eyes;
But soon, freed from the snare, with nimble feet
The tremblers bound to some more safe retreat.
The simple maniac starts, and finds, amazed,
The vision vanish'd which his fancy raised.

* * * * *

'Tis night—and darkness, black as Lailí's tresses,
Veils all around, and all his soul oppresses;
No lucid moon like Lailí's face appears;
No glimpse of light the gloomy prospect cheers:
In a rude cavern he despairing lies,
The tedious moments only mark'd with sighs.

XI.

Behold, what clouds of dust emerge
From the lone desert's distant verge!
And, high in dusky eddies driven,
Obscure the azure hue of heaven:
And now the tramp of steeds is heard,
And now the leader's angry word—
Now nearer, more distinct they grow—
Who is that leader?—friend or foe?
Alas! 'tis Lailí's vanquish'd sire,
Returning home, his heart on fire;
For though he has survived the blow,
Still burns the disgrace of his overthrow.

His tale is told: some Diw or Ghoul
Had palsied his intrepid soul,
And held his arm by magic foul,
Or potion from the enchanter's bowl;
Else had he driven, with easy hand,
The miscreant Noufal from the land;
For when did ever braggart lord
Fail, but when magic held his sword?

Now, shielded by the harem screen,
The sweet Narcissus sad is seen:
Listening she hears, disconsolate,
Her father's words, which seal her fate;

And what has Lailí now to bear,
But loneliness, reproach, despair,
With no congenial spirit to impart
One single solace to her bursting heart!

Meanwhile the spicy gale on every side
Wafts the high vaunting of her beauty's pride
Through all the neighbouring tribes, and more remote
Her name is whisper'd and her favor sought.
Suitors with various claims appear—the great,
The rich, the powerful—all impatient wait
To know for whom the father keeps that rare
But fragile crystal with such watchful care.
Her charms eclipse all others of her sex,
Given to be loved, but rival hearts to vex;
For when the lamp of joy illumes her cheeks,
The lover smiles, and yet his heart it breaks:
The full-blown rose thus sheds its fragrance round;
But there are thorns, not given to charm, but wound.
Among the rest that stripling came,
Who had before avow'd his flame;
His cheerful aspect seem'd to say,
For him was fix'd the nuptial-day.

His offerings are magnificent;
Garments embroider'd every fold,
And rarest gems, to win consent,
And carpets work'd with silk and gold:

Amber, and pearls, and rubies bright,
And bags of musk, attract the sight;
And camels of unequall'd speed,
And ambling nags of purest breed;—
These (resting for a while) he sends
Before him, and instructs his friends,
With all the eloquence and power
Persuasion brings in favoring hour,
To magnify his worth, and prove
That he alone deserves her love.—
"A youth of royal presence, Yemen's boast,
Fierce as a lion, powerful as a host;
Of boundless wealth, and valor's self, he wields
His conquering sword amid embattled fields.
Call ye for blood? 'tis shed by his own hand.
Call ye for gold? he scatters it like sand."

And when the flowers of speech their scent had shed,
Diffusing honors round the suitor's head;
Exalting him to more than mortal worth,
In person manly, noble in his birth;
The sire of Lailí seem'd oppressed with thought,
As if with some repulsive feeling fraught;
Yet promptly was the answer given—he soon
Decreed the fate of Yemen's splendid moon;
Saddled the steed of his desire, in sooth,
Flung his own offspring in the dragon's mouth.

Forthwith the nuptial pomp, the nuptial rites,
  Engage the chieftain's household—every square
Rings with the rattling drums—whose noise excites
  More deafening clamor through the wide bazár.
The pipe and cymbal, shrill and loud,
Delight the gay assembled crowd;
And all is mirth and jollity,
With song, and dance, and revelry.

But Lailí, mournful, sits apart,
The shaft of misery through her heart;
And black portentous clouds are seen
Darkening her soft expressive mien:
Her bosom swells with heavy sighs,
Tears gush from those heart-winning eyes,
Where Love's triumphant witchery lies.
In blooming spring a wither'd leaf,
She droops in agony of grief;
Loving her own—her only one—
Loving Majnún, and him alone;
All else from her affections gone;
And to be joined, in a moment's breath,
To another!—Death, and worse than death!

Soon as the sparkling stars of night
Had disappear'd, and floods of light
Shed from the morn's refulgent beam
Empurpled Dijla's rolling stream,

The bridegroom, joyous, rose to see
The bride equipp'd as bride should be:
The litter, and the golden throne,
Prepared for her to rest upon:
But what avails the tenderest care,
The fondest love, when dark despair
And utter hatred fill the breast
Of her to whom that fondness is address'd?
Quickly her sharp disdain the bridegroom feels,
And from her scornful presence shrinks and reels:
A solemn oath she takes, and cries,
With frenzy flashing from her eyes,—
"Hop'st thou I ever shall be thine?
It is my father's will, not mine!
Rather than be that thing abhorr'd,
My life-blood shall distain thy sword.
Away! nor longer seek to gain
A heart foredoom'd to endless pain;
A heart, no power of thine can move;
A bleeding heart, which scorns thy love!"

When Ibn Salám her frenzied look beheld,
And heard her vows, his cherish'd hopes were quell'd.
He soon perceived what art had been employ'd,—
All his bright visions faded and destroy'd;—
And found, when love has turn'd a maiden's brain,
Father and mother urge their power in vain.

XII.

The Arab poets who rehearse
Their legends in imperishable verse,
Say, when Majnún these tidings knew,
More wild, more moody wild, he grew;
Raving through wood and mountain glen;
Flying still more the haunts of men.

Sudden a perfume, grateful to the soul,
O'er his awaken'd senses stole.
He thought from Lailí's fragrant couch it came,
And filled with joy his wearied frame.
Ecstatic with the unexpected pleasure,
The fond memorial of his dearest treasure,
He sank upon the ground, beneath the shade
Of a broad palm, in senseless torpor laid.
  A stranger, quickly passing by,
Observed the love-lorn wanderer lie
Sleeping, or dead, and check'd his camel's pace
To mark the features of his face.
Loud roaring, like a demon, he awoke
The maniac from his trance, and gaily spoke:—
"Up, up, thou sluggard! up and see,
What thy heart's-ease has done for thee!
Better drive feeling from thy mind,
Since there's no faith in womankind:

Better be idle, than employ'd
In fruitless toil; better avoid
A mistress, though of form divine,
If she be fair and false as thine!
They 've given her charms to one as young—
The bride-veil o'er her brow is flung:
Close, side by side, from morn till night,
Kissing and dalliance their delight;
Whilst thou from human solace flying,
With unrequited love art dying.
—Distant from her adorer's view,
One in a thousand may be true:
The pen which writes, as if it knew
A woman's promise, splits in two.
While in another's warm embrace,
No witness to thy own disgrace,
Faithless, she wastes no thought on thee,
Wrapp'd in her own felicity.
Woman's desire is more intense
Than man's—more exquisite her sense;
But, never blinded by her flame,
Gain and fruition are her aim,
A woman's love is selfish all;
Possessions, wealth, secure her fall.
How many false and cruel prove,
And not one faithful in her love!
A contradiction is her life;
Without, all peace; within, all strife;

A dangerous friend, a fatal foe,
Prime breeder of a world of woe.
When we are joyous, she is sad;
When deep in sorrow, she is glad.
Such is the life a woman leads,
And in her sorcery still succeeds."

These words confused the lover's brain;
Fire ran through every swelling vein:
Frantic he dash'd his forehead on the ground,
And blood flow'd trickling from the ghastly wound.
"What added curse is this?" he groaning said,—
"Another tempest, roaring round my head!"

Whenever did a bleeding heart
  Betray no sign of blighted reason?
Can the most skilful gardener's art
  Still keep his flowers or fruit in season?
No; hearts dissolved in grief give birth
To madness, as the teeming earth
Yields herbs; and yet bewilder'd mind,
To all but one bright object blind,
Suffers no censure from the seer
Who guides the faithful Moslem here.
Love sanctifies the erring thought,
And Heaven forgives the deed by frenzy wrought.

"A rose, a lovely rose, I found,
With thorns and briers encompass'd round;
And, struggling to possess that prize,
The gardener in his wrath denies,
Behold my heart, all torn and bleeding,
Its pangs all other pangs exceeding:
I see the leaves expand and bloom,
I smell its exquisite perfume;
Its color, blushing in the light,
Gives to my raptured soul delight:
I weep beneath the cypress-tree,
And still the rose is not for me.
Alas! none hear, nor mark my moan;
Pride of my soul, my rose, is gone!
Another has, in open day,
Borne the heart-winning prize away.
Though wrapp'd in sweetest innocence,
The fell oppressor snatch'd her thence.
But who deserves the curse that 's sped
Upon the foul betrayer's head?
The gardener, in his lust for gold,
That rose—the boast of Irem—sold.

"Poor wretch! if worlds of wealth were mine,
Full willingly I 'd make them thine;
But not a dirhem for that rose,
The fatal cause of all my woes.

I would not play a villain's part,
And buy with gold a woman's heart;
'Tis not in gold to purchase love,
Above all wealth, all price above;
For I would rather die than see
A smile on lips that are not free.
Give me the boundless swell of bliss,
The heart upspringing to the kiss,
When life, and soul, and breath combine
To tell me, she is only mine;
The flood of joy o'erwhelming quite
My glowing senses with delight.
—Base wretch! and thou that rose hast sold:
A demon's curse upon thy gold."

The traveller witness'd with surprise
  How he the maniac's heart had wrung—
What remedy could he devise?
  He from his camel sprung;
And when the sufferer seem'd to be restored,
Forgiveness anxiously implored:—
" 'Twas wrong, and I deserve the blame;
I mark'd with infamy her name:
My fault is of the darkest hue,—
My crime—for Lailí still is true!
What! though in nuptial band united,
Her faith, to thee so often plighted,

Spotless remains, still firm, unbroken,
As proved by many a mournful token.
For every moment's space can claim
A thousand recollections of thy name:
Thus ever present to her memory,
She lives, and only lives for thee.
One year has pass'd since she was made a bride;
But what of years? whatever may betide,
Were it a thousand, still her heart's the same,
Unchanged, unchangeable her earliest cherish'd flame."

Now Majnún, desolate, his fate perceived,
  As in a glass, the misery of his lot,
And, from the first impression scarce relieved,
  Felt his abandonment, and only not forgot.

Wasted and wan, he flutter'd where he lay;
  And, turning to that magic point which led
To where his angel-face was wont to stay,
  Thus, in a melancholy tone, he said:—

"Alas! my passion glow'd in every part;
Thine in thy tongue, but never in thy heart;
With thy new love hast thou so amorous grown?
And am I worthless as a desert-stone?
What is a word, a promise, oath, or pledge?
Mockery, which never can the heart engage.

What was my garden's wealth but fruit and flowers?
And all that wealth a raven now devours;
And what has been my constant care and toil,
But for another to prepare the spoil?
When first my soul was destined to be thine,
I little thought that treasure to resign;
Think of thy broken vows, to what they tend;
Think of thy falsehood, and lament its end.
My doom is fix'd; my choice no longer free;
My martyr-life devoted still to thee!"

XIII.

Meantime, the father mourn'd his wretched state,
Like Jacob o'er his Joseph's unknown fate;
No rest by day, no sleep by night;
Grief o'er him shed its withering blight;
Incessant yawnings wrung his heart,
  He sat in darkness, silent, lone:
"Why did my child from home depart?
  Where has the hopeless wanderer gone?"
Dreading that death's relentless dart
  His best-beloved had overthrown.

Sudden he rose—despair gave force
  And vigor to his aged frame;
And, almost frantic with remorse,
  Gathering upon himself the blame,

He trod the maze of wood and wild,
Seeking his poor forsaken child;
And when the day withdrew its light,
He pass'd in cavern rude the night;
But never ceased his venturous quest—
No peace for him—no strengthening rest.
In vain he paced the desert round,
For not a trace of him was found.
At length a herdsman, falling in his way,
Described the spot where Majnún lay;
Craggy, and deep, and terrible to view,
It seem'd a grave all damp with noxious dew.
Thither proceeding, by the stranger led,
He finds with horror that sepulchral bed;
And, fearful of the worst, beholds the wreck
Of his once-lovely boy;—
He sees a serpent winding round his neck,
Playful, not destined to destroy:
It stays but for a moment—all around,
Limbs half-devour'd, and bones, bestrew the ground.
With cautious step descending, he surveys
Th' unconscious youth, who meets his anxious gaze
With a wild look, which could not recognise
The tottering form before him—"Who art thou?
And what thy errand?" The old man replies—
"I am thy father! I have found thee now,
After long search!" Embracing, both remain'd
In deep compassionate sorrow, fondly strain'd

Each to the other's bosom; and when he,
The maniac, had regain'd his memory,
And beams of light burst through his 'nighted brain,
And he beheld and knew his sire again,
Joy sparkled in his faded eye awhile,
And his parch'd lips seem'd curl'd into a smile.
The poor old father said, with feeble voice,
"Thou mak'st my heart both tremble and rejoice:
The path o'er which thy feet are doom'd to pass
Shows blades of swords, not harmless blades of grass;
And I would warn thee never more to roam;
Thy only safety is to stay at home.
Dogs have a home, and thou hast none to boast:
Art thou a man to human comfort lost?
If man thou art, then like a man appear,
Or, if a demon, be a demon here.
The ghoul, created to perplex the earth,
Is still a ghoul, and answers to its birth;
But thou 'rt a man; and why, with human soul,
Forget thy nature and become a ghoul?
To-day, if thou shouldst throw the reins aside,
To-morrow thou may'st ask, and be denied.
Soon shall I pass away, and be at rest;
No longer this frail world's unhappy guest.
My day is mingling with the shades of night;
My life is losing all its wonted light.
Soul of thy father! re-inspired with grace,
Rise, and protect the honors of thy race!

That, ere this frame be in the grave laid low,
I may the guardian of my birthright know;
That, ere I die, to soothe a parent's grief,
Thou mayst be hail'd in thine own home, the chief.
Forbid it, Heaven, that when my hour is past,
My house and home should to the winds be cast!
That plundering strangers, with rapacious hand,
Should waste my treasure and despoil my land!
And Heaven forbid, that both at once should fall,
(My greatest dread) and thus extinguish all!
That when the summons reaches me to die,
Thy death should also swell the funeral cry!"

These words sank deep in Majnún's breast: he seem'd
Alter'd in mood, as through his senses stream'd
The memory of his home, the fond regard
Of his dear mother, and the joys he shared
From her affection. Days and nights he tried,
To banish from his thoughts another's bride:
Repentance came, and oft the strife renew'd,
But tyrant love that feeling soon subdued;
(Love, a wild elephant in might, which grows
More powerful when opposed by friends or foes;)
And the poor maniac thus his sire address'd:—
"Thy counsel, father, is the wisest, best;
And I would gladly to thy wish conform:
But what am I? a helpless wretch, a worm,
Without the power to do what I approve,
Enslaved, the victim of almighty love.

To me the world is swallow'd up—I see
Nothing but Lailí—all is lost to me,
Save her bright image—father, mother, home,
All buried in impenetrable gloom,
Beyond my feeling;—yet I know thou 'rt here,
And I could weep;—but what avails the tear,
Even were it at a father's funeral shed?
For human sorrows never reach the dead.
Thou say'st, the night of Death is on thee falling!
Then must I weep, thy fostering care recalling;
But I shall die in utter misery,
And none be left in life to weep for me."
  Syd Omri, with unutterable grief,
Gazed on his son, whose sorrows mock'd relief;
And, hopeless, wretched, every thought resign'd
That once was balm and comfort to his mind.
Then, showering blessings o'er his offspring's head,
  Groaning, he parted from that dismal cave;
And, wrapt in deepest anguish, homeward sped;
  But 'twas alas! to his expected grave.
Gently he sank, by age and grief oppress'd,
From this vain world, to that of endless rest.
Vain world indeed! who ever rested here?
The lustrous moon hath its eternal sphere;
But man, who in this mortal prison sighs,
Appears like lightning, and like lightning flies.
  A pilgrim-step approach'd the wild retreat,
Where Majnún linger'd in his rocky seat,

And the sad tale was told. He fell
Upon the earth insensible;
And, grovelling, with a frantic air,
His bosom beat—he tore his hair,
And never rested, night or day,
Till he had, wandering far away,
Reach'd the sad spot where peaceful lay
His father's bones, now crumbling with decay.
His arms around the grave he flung,
And to the earth delirious clung;
Grasping the ashes of the dead,
He cast them o'er his prostrate head,
And, with repentant tears, bedew'd
The holy relics round him strew'd.
O'erwhelming was the sharpen'd sense
Of his contrition, deep, intense;
And sickness wrapp'd his shatter'd frame
In a slow fever's parching flame;
Still, ceaseless, 'twas his wont to rave
Upon his father's sacred grave.
He felt the bitterness of fate;
He saw his folly now too late;
And worlds would give again to share
His generous father's constant care;
For he had oft, in wanton guise,
Contemn'd the counsels of the wise;
Had with a child's impatience burn'd,
And scorn for sympathy return'd;

And now, like all of human mould,
When the indulgent heart is cold,
Which would have seal'd his happiness,
He mourns—but mourns his own distress;
For, when the diamond blazed like day,
He cast it recklessly away.

XIV.

Who wanders near that palmy glade,
Where the fresh breeze adds coolness to the shade?
'Tis Majnún;—he has left his father's tomb,
Again 'mid rocks and scorching plains to roam,
Unmindful of the sun's meridian heat,
Or the damp dewy night, with unshod feet;
Unmindful of the forest's savage brood,
Howling on every side in quest of blood;
No dread has he from aught of earth or air,
From den or eyry, calm in his despair:
He seems to court new perils, and can view
With unblench'd visage scenes of darkest hue;
Yet is he gentle, and his gracious mien
Checks the extended claw, where blood has been;
For tiger, wolf, and panther, gather round
The maniac as their king, and lick the ground;
Fox and hyena fierce their snarling cease;
Lion and fawn familiar meet in peace;
Vulture and soaring eagle, on the wing,
Around his place of rest their shadows fling;

Like Suliman, o'er all extends his reign;
His pillow is the lion's shaggy mane;
The wily leopard, on the herbage spread,
Forms like a carpet his romantic bed:
And lynx and wolf, in harmony combined,
Frisk o'er the sward, and gambol with the hind.
All pay their homage with respect profound,
As if in circles of enchantment bound.

Among the rest, one little fawn
Skipp'd nimbly o'er the flowery lawn;
And, beautifully delicate,
Sprang where the admiring maniac sate:
So soft, so meek, so sweetly mild,
So shy, so innocently wild,
And, ever playful in his sight,
The fondling grew his great delight;
He loved its pleasing form to trace,
And kiss its full black eyes and face,
Thinking of Lailí all the while;
For fantasies the heart beguile;
And with th' illusive dream impress'd,
He hugg'd the favorite to his breast:
With his own hand the fawn he fed,
And choicest herbs before it spread;
And all the beasts assembled there
Partook of his indulgent care,

And, day and night, they, unconstrain'd,
In wondrous harmony remain'd.
And thus, throughout the world, we find
'Mid brutes, as well as humankind,
A liberal hand, a friendly voice,
Bids e'en the savage heart rejoice.
There is a curious story told
Of a despotic king, of old,
Which proves ferocious beasts endued
With a deep sense of gratitude.
The king had in his palace-bounds
A den of man-devouring hounds;
And all on whom his anger fell
Were cast into that dreadful cell.
Among the courtiers there was one,
For wisdom, wit, and shrewdness known,
Long in the royal household nursed,
But still he always fear'd the worst,
Thinking the fatal day might come
For him to share an equal doom;
And therefore, by a dexterous scheme,
His life endeavour'd to redeem.
Unseen, by night, he often stood
And fed the hounds with savoury food;
And well their bounteous friend they knew,
And in their hearts attachment grew;
When, just as he, prophetic, thought,
The king his death unfeeling sought;

Sternly his good old courtier blamed,
And to the ravenous dogs condemn'd.
'Twas night when in the den he cast
His victim for a dog's repast:
Next morn, unshamed by such a deed,
(Dooming the innocent to bleed,)
He sent a page to look for him,
Torn, he expected, limb from limb:
The wondering keeper, who obey'd
The king, and not a trice delay'd,
Now, hastening to the presence, cried,
"O king! his virtue has been tried;
He bears an angel's blessed charm,
And God protects his life from harm:
Untouch'd, though fetter'd fast, I found him,
The dogs all fondly fawning round him!"
The king was struck with wonderment
At this miraculous event;
And seeing, in that horrid cell,
The guiltless courtier safe and well,
He ask'd, with tears profusely shed,
By what strange spell he was not dead?
"No juggling words had I to say;
I fed the bloodhounds every day;
And thence their gratitude arose,
Which saved me from my cruel foes.
But I have served thee many a year,
And for it thou has sent me here!

A dog has feeling—thou hast none—
A dog is thankful for a bone;
But thou, with hands in blood imbrued,
Hast not one spark of gratitude."
Abash'd the despot saw his crimes,
And changed his frightful course betimes.

XV.

Sweet slumber had diffused the charm of rest
Through the poor maniac's agitated breast,
And as the morn, magnificently bright,
Pour'd o'er the cloudless sky its purple light,
The smiling presage of a prosperous day,
He rose refresh'd, and hail'd the heavenly ray.
Graceful he stood amidst the varied herd,
And, warm'd with hope, his orisons preferr'd;
When suddenly a horseman met his view,
Who, as it seem'd, the wandering lover knew.
"Romantic youth! I see the timorous deer
And the fierce lion meet in concord here,
And thou the monarch—strange! but mark! I bear
A secret tale of one, so loved, so fair.
What wouldst thou feel, did I her name declare?
What is the cypress to her form divine?
What is the perfume from a martyr's shrine?
What, should that idol's fate be mix'd with thine?
Her ringlets twisted like the graceful Jím,
Her shape an Alif, and her mouth a Mím;

Her eyes like two Narcissuses, that grow
Where the pure waters of a fountain flow;
Her eyebrows, join'd, a double arch express;
Her beauteous cheeks an angel might caress.
But what can I of such perfection say?
How to the blind Creation's charms portray?
I saw her weep—the tear-drops glistening fell
In showers from eyes which their own tale could tell;
And yet I ask'd for whom she wept and mourn'd—
For one untrue, or one to dust return'd?
Opening her ruby lips, she softly said—
'My heart is desolate—my joys are fled;
I once was Lailí—need I more reveal?
Worse than a thousand maniacs now I feel:
More wild than that dark star which rules my fate,
More mad than Majnún's my distracted state.
If that dark spirit thou shouldst haply find—
That mournful wreck of an enlighten'd mind—
How wilt thou recognise him? By that sad
Disorder'd aspect, oft pronounced as mad;
By that unutterable grief which preys
Upon his heart; that melancholy gaze,
Which has no sense of outward things; that love
So pure, an emanation from above.
O that I could escape this wretched thrall,
And leave, for ever leave, my father's hall.
But go, and seek the wanderer;—glen and cave
Patient explore—his refuge, or his grave:

Find him; and, faithful, with unwearied feet
Return, and tell me his forlorn retreat.'

Silent I heard her earnest prayer;
Mark'd her desponding voice and air;
And while she still, in tenderest mood,
Bedew'd with tears, before me stood,
The story of thy woes, which long
Had been the theme of many a song,
Familiar to the country round,
I sang, and deep affection found;
So deep, that sigh, succeeding sigh,
She trembled in her agony,
And, senseless, sank upon the ground,
Where pale and motionless she lay
As if her life had ebb'd away.
But soon as that dread swoon was o'er,
And sobs and tears relieved her heart;
Again she press'd me to restore
Him she adored—'If kind thou art,
And kind thou must be to a wretch forlorn,
I feel thou wouldst not play a traitor's part;
Thou canst not view my misery with scorn.
Alas! though I may seem to him untrue,
Pity is still to woman's sorrows due.'

Her rosy fingers press
The written tale of her distress;

And, raising to her ruby mouth
That passionate record of her truth,
Kiss'd it a thousand times, and shed
A flood of tears, whilst mournfully she said—
'To him this sad memorial give—
To him for whom alone I live.'"
Majnún, perplex'd, with painful feelings riven,
Seem'd to refuse what still to him was Heaven;
Imputed falsehood swept across his mind,
But left no dark distrustful thoughts behind.
At length, the writing eagerly he took;
But, as he read, he falter'd, wept, and shook.
Adoring the Creator, she began—
"Beyond the praise of tongue, to mortal man
His love and goodness,"—thus her *námeh* ran—
"He with the light of wisdom cheers the soul;
He bids the cheek to glow, the eye to roll,
And every mortal bends to his control.
To this, he scatters jewels bright and rare,
To that, good sense to strive with worldly care:
To me he gave the love which time defies—
The love I bear thee, spotless from the skies;
Fountain of Khizer, sparkling in the shade!
Fountain of life to thine own Arab maid!
In truth and love to thee my heart was given,—
That truth and love remain, the gift of Heaven.
Though far from thee—a wife against my will,
I am thine own affianced partner still:

Still single—still, in purity and faith,
Thine own unchanged—unchangeable in death.
Thou 'rt all the world to me—the very earth
Thou tread'st on is to me of matchless worth;
Yet in a different sphere my race is run;
I am the moon, and thou the radiant sun:
By destiny thus sunder'd—how can I
Merit reproach, who at thy feet would die?
Since thus divided, pity thou my lot,
With all thy vows and raptures unforgot;
Life's sweetest flow'rets, in their brightest bloom,
Turn'd to the bitterness of fell *Zikúm.*"

Yes, Majnún wept and shook; and now
What answer could he frame, and how?
A wanderer, destitute—no reed,
No tablets, to supply his need—
But Lailí's messenger had brought
The means—and thus the maniac wrote:—
"To him who form'd the starry throne
Of heaven, and rules the world alone;
Who, in the dark mysterious mine,
Maketh the unseen diamond shine;
Who thus on human life bestows
The gem which in devotion glows;
To him be gratitude and praise,
The constant theme of Moslem lays!

—A burning heart, in sorrow deep,
What can it do but sigh and weep?
And what can this memorial bear
To thee, but wailings of despair?
I am the dust beneath thy feet,
Though destined never more to meet.
Thy beauty is my Kâba shrine,
The arc of heaven, for ever mine;
Garden of Irem—hid from me,
The Paradise I must not see;
Yet thou hast quench'd my genial light;
My day is now like blackest night.
With fondness on thy flattering tongue
Thou smilest, and my heart is wrung;
For those whose tongues are gentlest found
Are wont to give the deadliest wound.
The lily's petals oft appear
As fatal as the sword or spear.
She, whom 'twas rapture to behold,
Could she be basely bought and sold?
Couldst thou to me thy promise break,
And spurn me for another's sake?
Acting a bland deceiver's part,
And solacing another's heart!
But, peace!—no more of thoughts so sad,
Or I shall grow intensely mad;
I yearn no more those lips to press;—
But is the joy of memory less?

The morning-breeze thy fragrance brings;
And up my heart exulting springs;
Still more when I reflecting see
How once the cup was fill'd by thee.
O Heaven! how rapturous to receive
That which forbids the heart to grieve;
To sit with thee in amorous play,
And quaff the ruby every day;
To kiss those lips, all honey-dew,
Of liquid bright cornelian hue!
O! could I kiss them once again!
The fancy fires my wilder'd brain.
—Need I the painter's art to trace
The lineaments of thy angel face?
No—they 're indelibly impress'd
Within my ever-faithful breast.
'Tis ours, divided, to deplore
Scenes we can never witness more;
But, though on earth denied to rest,
Shall we not both in heaven be bless'd?"

* * * * *

Majnún's distracted state was not unknown
Where to the wretched kindness could be shown;
—A wealthy chieftain (Selim was his name),
Whose generous deeds had won the world's acclaim;
Whose heart was still on others' woes engaged—
He heal'd their wounds, their anguish he assuaged;

Raiment and various food had oft supplied,
Where'er the love-lorn wanderer might abide.
Mounted upon his rapid steed, one day,
He sought the distant place where Majnún lay;
And him at length, with placid mien, he found
By herds of forest-beasts encompass'd round.
Fearful of savage natures, he retired,
'Til Majnún, beckoning, confidence inspired;
And then, approaching near, he told his name,
And recognised him, though his wasted frame
Seem'd an uncoffin'd corse. Ashamed, he said —
"O let these robes thy naked body shade,
These robes for thee brought hither." "Not for me;
I want no covering,—without clothes I 'm free.
Behold these tatter'd fragments, thrown aside;
These once were robes, and once my foolish pride."
But, press'd again, those tatters he resumed,
And sat like one to death and darkness doom'd.—
Now savoury viands were before him spread,
But not a morsel raised he to his head;
He turn'd him round, and, scorning the repast,
To his familiars all the banquet cast.
Then Selim asked—"What is thy food, my friend?
Without support, thy life must quickly end."
—"My spirit's freshness, and its secret power,
Come from the breeze which marks the morning-hour;
Yes, every zephyr from my mistress brings
Life to the soul upon its fragrant wings;

When hunger presses, from the weeping trees
I gather gums, its cravings to appease;
And herbs and grass, and the transparent rill,
Support me in the state thou seest me still;
But though thy proffer'd food regale not me,
The beasts around enjoy'd the banquetry;
And if I sought on living thing to feed,
Birds might be caught; but I detest the deed;
And he who is contented grass to eat,
Defies the world—the world is at his feet;
For what can pomp, and wealth, and feasts avail?
I live on grass:—but hear the Záhid's tale.

In ancient times a king, they say,
Through a wild forest took his way;
And marking, as along he rode,
A Záhid's desolate abode,
Ask'd his attendants if they knew
What the Recluse was wont to do;
What was his food, and where he slept,
And why remote from man he kept.—
A courtier towards the Záhid ran,
And soon brought forth that holy man;—
"And wherefore dost thou pass thy days
Shunning the world's inviting ways,
Choosing this dismal wretched hole,
Grave of the body and the soul?"

—"I have no friends to love me—none;
No power, except to live alone."
Then, where his fawns in quiet fed,
Took up some blades of grass, and said—
"This is my food—this, want supplies!"
The courtier look'd with scornful eyes,
And answer'd,—"Taste but royal food,
And thou 'lt not fancy grass so good."
"Indeed!" the Záhid said, and smiled,
"That is a sad mistake, my child!
Worldlings are still to luxury prone;
To thee its sweetness is unknown;
Stranger to such delicious fare,
No doubt thou 'rt charm'd with food more rare!"
—Soon as this speech the monarch heard,
Noting, attentive, every word,
And wondering such a seer to meet,
Fell at the pious Záhid's feet,
And kiss'd the greensward, as he knelt
Where that contented hermit dwelt.

XVI.

O'er Majnún's spirit, long in darkness cast,
A fitful gleam of homeward feeling pass'd;
And now he asks for friends he once preferr'd,
Asks for his mother, broken-winged bird;
And wishes e'en to visit home again—
As if the maddening fire had left his brain.

Selim at this brief glimpse of reason caught,
And to his mother's distant mansion brought
Without delay the wanderer. Deep her grief
To see how wither'd was that verdant leaf—
To see the red rose faded from his cheek,
His eye so alter'd, and his frame so weak;
From head to foot she kisses him, and weeps;
His hair, all matted, in her tears she steeps,
And clasps him fondly to her beating heart,
As if she never from her boy would part:—
"My darling child! the love-game thou hast play'd
Has thus, alas! reduced thee to a shade;
In that encounter sad of mortal scathe
Thou grasp'dst the two-edged scimitar of death.
Thy father gone, his troubles all are past,
Heart-broken man! and I shall follow fast.
Arise! and enter thy own mansion here;
Come, 'tis thy own sweet home, and doubly dear—
Thy nest;—and birds, though distant in their flight,
Always return to their own nests at night.
While yet an infant in thy cradle-bed,
I watch'd thy slumber, pillow'd thy sweet head;
And canst thou now that mother's fondness see,
And mark without remorse her love for thee?
Refuse the joy thy presence can impart,
And cast a shadow o'er her drooping heart?"

A cloud again obscured the orb of day—
Again his wavering intellect gave way;

"Mother, there is no hope—the time is past;
With gloom eternal is my fate o'ercast;
No fault of mine—no crime, to press me down—
But all my countless woes to thee are known;
Like a poor bird within its cage immured,
My soul has long this prison-life endured.
Ask me not, mother, to remain at home;
For there, to me, no peace can ever come.
Oh, better will it be for me to stray
'Mid mountain-glens, and herd with beasts of prey,
Than linger on a spot where human care
Only augments my misery and despair."
He ceased, and kiss'd his mother's feet, and fled
Precipitate along the path which led
To the wild mountains. Dreadful was the stroke!
The mother's heart, like the old father's, broke;
In Death's cold ocean, wave thus follows wave;
And thus she follow'd to the silent grave.
Selim again the maniac's haunts explored,
Again supplied his frugal board,
And, with a mournful voice, the tale reveal'd—
Father and mother gone,
Himself now left alone,
Sole heir—his doom of desolation seal'd—
He beat his brows, and from his eyes
Fell tears of blood; his piercing cries
Rang through the forest, and again,
Pouring the saddest, wildest strain,

He hasten'd from his gloomy cave,
To weep upon his mother's grave.
But when that paroxysm of grief—
That agony intense, but brief—
Had, like a whirlwind, pass'd away,
  And left him in a milder mood,
To love and Lailí still a prey,
  He trod again his mountain-solitude:
For what to him was hoarded store,
The wealth of parents now no more?
Had he not long, ill-fated one!
Abandon'd all for love alone?

XVII.

Lailí meanwhile had read and seen
What Majnún's thoughts had ever been;
And though her plighted faith seem'd broken,
From him she held the tenderest token:
Deep in her heart, a thousand woes
Disturb'd her days' and nights' repose:
A serpent at its very core,
Writhing and gnawing evermore;
And no relief—a prison-room
Being now the lovely sufferer's doom.
—Fate look'd at last with favouring eye;
The night was dark, no watchman nigh;
And she had gain'd the outer gate,
Where, shrouded, unobserved, she sate,

Gazing on every side to find
Some friend to calm her troubled mind;
When, welcome as a cherish'd guest,
A holy seer her vision bless'd,
Who, ever, like an angel, strove
The heart's deep anguish to remove;
Who lived to succour the distress'd,
To soothe and staunch the bleeding breast:
To him she spake—"In pity hear,
A wretch distraught with love and fear!
Know'st thou the youth, of peerless grace,
Who mingles with the forest-race,
Savage or tame, and fills the air,
Alas! for me, with his despair?"
—"Yes, lovely moon!" he answer'd,—"well I know
That hapless wanderer, and his cureless woe;
Lailí still on his tongue, the Arab maid
He ceaseless seeks through every bower and glade,
Unconscious of the world, its bloom or blight,
Lailí alone for ever in his sight."

The Arab maiden wept, and cried,—"No more!
I am the cause, and I his loss deplore;
Both have our sorrows, both are doom'd to feel
The wounds of absence, which will never heal;
For me he roams through desert wild and drear,
While Fate condemns me to be fetter'd here!"
—Then from her ear a lustrous gem she drew,
Which, having kiss'd, she to the hermit threw,—

And said,—"Forbid it I should ask in vain!
Let these fond eyes behold his face again!
But caution must control the zeal you show:
Some signal must be given, that I may know
When he is nigh—some stanzas of his own
Warbled beneath my casement, where, alone,
I sit and watch—for secret must we be,
Or all is lost to Majnún and to me!"
—Within his girdle-fold the smiling saint
Placed the rich gem, and on his errand went.
But did no obstacle his task oppose?
A thousand, daily, in his progress rose:
Where'er his arduous course he anxious urged,
Perplexing paths in various lines diverged;
Through tangled glens, the ground with creepers spread,
Meshes of shadowy branches o'er his head,
Now a wide plain before him—mountains grey,
And now an emerald greensward cheer'd his way:
At last, upon a hillock's shady side,
The long-sought love-sick wanderer he descried,
By forest-beasts surrounded,—in a ring,
Like guards appointed to protect their king.
Majnún perceived him, and with upraised hand
Made his wild followers at a distance stand;
And then the seer approach'd—his homage paid—
"O thou, unmatch'd in love!" he kindly said,

"Lailí, the world and beauty's queen,
Who long has thy adorer been;
And many a year has run its race,
Since she has seen that pensive face—
Since she has heard that tuneful voice
Which ever made her heart rejoice:
And now, at her command, I bear
Her earnest, almost dying, prayer.
She longs to see thee once again,
To sit with thee and soothe thy pain;
To feel, on pleasure's downy wings,
The joy a lover's presence brings.
And wilt thou not, with equal glee,
Behold thyself from bondage free?
The Grove of Palms thy feet must trace,
Near Lailí's rural dwelling-place.
That is the promised spot; and thou
Wilt there receive both pledge and vow,
And sing, with voice subdued and clear,
Thy sweetest ghazel in her ear."
Majnún uprose with joyous look,
And for his guide the hermit took:
And, passing quick the space between,
Arrived at that romantic scene
Where the majestic palms display'd
A cool, refreshing depth of shade;

And there the tribes of wood and plain,
Which form'd the wanderer's vassal-train,
Promptly as human retinue,
To an adjoining copse withdrew.

The seer, advancing with a cautious pace,
To the pavilion of that angel-face—
That star of beauty—that sweet silvery moon—
Whisper'd the presence of her own Majnún.
But woman's mind can from its purpose range,
And seem to change, without the power to change;
And thus she said—"Alas! it cannot be:
I must not meet him—such is Fate's decree;
The lamp thus lit, Love's temple to illume,
Will not enlighten, but the heart consume;
For I am wedded—to another given—
This worthless dust still in the view of Heaven;
And though compell'd—let others bear the blame!—
I was not born to sacrifice my fame.
Prudence forbids such perils should be mine;
Rather for ever let me here repine;
But faithful still, with his melodious tongue
How often have the sweetest echoes rung?
Yes, faithful still, he may upon mine ear
Chant the rich numbers which I love to hear:
Let him with nectar fill his luscious cup,
And, still adoring, I will drink it up."

Prostrate, in tears, upon a fountain's side,
The saint found Majnún, who impatient cried—
"What is this amber incense round me flying?
Is it the breath of spring o'er rose-buds sighing?
No—not the fragrance of the early spring—
Lailí's sweet locks alone such odours fling!
So powerful is the impulse they impart,
They fill with dying ecstasy my heart."
The saint, well-taught in love's mysterious lore,
Knew what it was the absent to deplore;
But said—"Thou canst not hope that she,
Unsought, unask'd, will come to thee!
Woman demands a warmer suit,
And none her sacred power dispute."

"Upbraid me not with maxim old—
Think'st thou that Majnún's suit is cold
When, from the very scent, I feel
Intoxication o'er me steal?
Must I the real bliss decline
And never taste the luscious wine?"
So saying, seated in that palmy grove,
To Lailí thus he breath'd his lay of love.
"O whither art thou gone?
And where am I?—alone!
Forsaken, lost—and what remains?
Life only creeping through my veins;

And yet that life is not my own,
But thine;—I only breathe to moan:
A thing of memory, to deplore
The past, since hope can smile no more.
Familiar to the pangs which scorn relief,
Grief smiles upon me, and I smile on grief.
Grief makes thee dearer still; for grief and thee
Seem of each other born. Grief paints to me
Thy matchless beauty:—without grief, no thought
Of thy perfections to my mind is brought.
O Heaven! that ever we were doom'd to part!—
We are but one—two bodies, and one heart.
As summer clouds with rain the meadows greet,
Majnún dissolves in sorrow at thy feet;
Whilst thy soft cheeks lend beauty to the sky,
Majnún, alas! is taught by them to die.
The bulbul o'er thy roses joyous stoops;
Majnún, from thee disjoin'd, divided, droops;
And whilst the world devotes itself to strife,
Majnún would sacrifice to thee his life.
O that kind fortune would our joys approve,
And yield the blessings of successful love!
The gorgeous moon, with her pellucid light,
Converting into dazzling day the night;
And we together seated, ear to ear,
The sparkling wine, our beverage, ever near;
I playing with those ringlets, which descend
In magic curls, and o'er thy shoulders bend;

Thou, with those dark and love-enkindling eyes,
In which the living spell of witchery lies,
Gazing in fondness on me. That sweet lip!
I see it the rich wine enamour'd sip:
I see us both—what happiness! and none
To drive the sovereign pleasure from his throne;
Nor shame, nor fear, to crush affection's flower,
Happy, unseen, in that sequester'd bower.
—But bring me wine! this bright illusion stay!
Wine! wine! keep sad realities away!
Wine, Saki, wine! the house without a light
Is but a prison, odious to the sight;
For broken hearts, immured in gloom like mine,
Are dungeon-dark, unbless'd with light or wine;
O God! preserve me from this endless night!
Give me one day of joy—one moment of delight!"
  Then strangely moved, he wildly closed his lay,
Sprung on his feet, and sudden burst away;
And Lailí, who had heard him, deeply mourn'd,
And, sad, to her secluded home return'd.

XVIII.

Through many a town and bower had spread
The maniac's tale—all anxious read
In Bagdad and far-distant plains
The mournful lover's amorous strains;

And every heart, which had been wrung
With wither'd hopes, in pity hung
O'er sorrows which to madness drove—
The very martyrdom of love.
And all aspired to seek the cave
Which hourly might become his grave;
To find th' enduring man; to view
That prodigy—but seen by few—
Of whom the world astonish'd spoke,
As crush'd beneath misfortune's yoke;
Whose truth and constancy excell'd
All that the world had e'er beheld.
A gallant youth, who long had known
  The pangs of love, impatient rose,
And on his camel, all alone,
  Sought for the man of many woes;
Anxious to be the first to see
The man pre-eminent in misery;
And many a farsang he had rode,
Before he reach'd the lover's wild abode.

Majnún beheld him from afar,
And sent his vassals to their lair;
And welcome gave, and ask'd his name,
And whence the hurrying stranger came.—
"I come, my friend, to make thee glad;
I come from beautiful Bagdad.

In that enchanting place I might
Have lived in transport day and night;
But I have heard thy tender lays,
Thy sorrows, which the world amaze;
And all that now remains for me
Is, all life long, to dwell with thee.
Thy tuneful strains such joy impart,
Each word is treasured in my heart:
In love, like thee, I weep and sigh—
Let us together live—together die!"

Astonish'd at this strange desire,
  Laughing, the maniac thus replies:—
"Sir knight! so soon does pleasure tire?
  And dost thou worldly pomp despise,
And all that luxury can give,
With me in wood and cave to live?

Mistaken youth! what dost thou know
  Of broken hearts—of love like mine—
That thou shouldst life's sweet joys forego,
  And every cheering hope resign?
I have companions, night and day;
But forest-inmates—beasts of prey;
Yet do I ask no other—none;
I 'd rather live with them alone.
What hast thou social seen in me,
When demons from my presence flee,

That thou wouldst brave the noon-tide heat,
  The dangers of the midnight air,
Unshelter'd, naked head and feet,
  To herd with one not worth thy care,
Nor worth a thought? Beneath the scorching sun
I thread the wild wood, and, when day is done,
Lie myself down upon a beggar's throne—
My canopy, the trees—my pillow, a rude stone.
Houseless and poor, and oft with hunger press'd,
How can I take a stranger for my guest?
Whilst thou, surrounded by thy friends at home,
Moved by no need, but by a whim to roam,
Mayst pass thy hours in cheerfulness and glee,
And never think of such a wretch as me!"
The gallant youth now placed in view
  Various refreshments he had thither brought—
Sweet cakes and fruit—and from his pannier drew
  Heart-easing wine, his purpose to promote,
To win the favor of the moon-struck man;
And thus his brief but earnest speech began:—
"Friend, share my meal in kindness, and allow
A smile of joy to clear that furrow'd brow!
In bread is life; it strengthens every part,
And, while it strengthens, cheers the drooping heart."
Majnún rejoin'd—"The argument is just;
Without refreshment man descends to dust:

Nerve, power, and strength, from nourishment proceed;
But this is not the nourishment I need."
"Yet mortals change, whate'er their aim;
Nothing on earth remains the same:
know thou canst not be unmoved;
For ever thus thou canst not be;
Perpetual change the heavens have proved;
And night and morn, successively,
Attest its truth. That thou hast loved
I know; but thou mayst yet be free;
The heavens are clothed in deepest gloom;
Black is the threatening day of doom;
The clouds fly off, the storm is past,
No longer howls the scattering blast;
The heavens resume their wonted sheen,
And brighter glows the varied scene:
So grief devours the heart awhile;
So frowns are follow'd by a smile:
Like thee, was I enchanted, bound,
Girt by love's galling fetters round;
But to the winds my grief I flung,
And to my fate no longer clung.
This fire of love, which burns so bright,
What is it but a treacherous light?
The type of youth;—when that is o'er,
The burning mountain flames no more!"

But Majnún spurn'd the traitor-thought, and said—
"Speak'st thou to me as one to feeling dead?
I am myself the king of love; and now
Glory in my dominion: and wouldst thou
Persuade me to abandon all that Heaven
Has, 'mid my sufferings, for my solace given,
To quit that cherish'd hope, than life more dear,
Which rivets me to earth, and keeps me here?
That pure ethereal love, that mystic flower,
Nurtured in Heaven, fit for an angel's dower?
What! from my heart expel the dream of love?
First from the ocean's bed the sands remove!
Useless the effort,—useless is thy aim,—
Thou canst not quench a never-dying flame.
Then cease persuasion. Why to me appear
A master, teaching, like some holy seer?
He who aspires to open locks, they say,
To be successful, first must know the way."
The youth perceived his error, yet remain'd
  In friendly converse a few fleeting days;
And, by the oracle of love enchain'd,
  Listen'd, enraptured, to his varied lays;
Companionship delectable! then rose
  To bid adieu, since there he might not stay,
And, sorrowing, left the man of many woes,
  Surrounded by his vassal-beasts of prey.

XIX.

How beautifully blue
 The firmament! how bright
The moon is sailing through
 The vast expanse, to-night!
And at this lovely hour
 The lonely Lailí weeps
Within her prison-tower,
 And her sad record keeps—

How many days, how many years,
 Her sorrows she has borne!
A lingering age of sighs and tears;
 A night that has no morn;
Yet in that guarded tower she lays her head,
Shut like a gem within its stony bed.
And who the warder of that place of sighs?
Her husband!—he the dragon-watch supplies.

What words are those which meet her anxious ear?
Unusual sounds, unusual sights appear;
Lamps flickering round, and wailings sad and low,
Seem to proclaim some sudden burst of woe.
Beneath her casement rings a wild lament,
Death-notes disturb the night; the air is rent
With clamorous voices; every hope is fled;
He breathes no longer—Ibn Salím is dead!

The fever's rage had nipp'd him in his bloom;
He sank unloved, unpitied, to the tomb.

And Lailí marks the moon; a cloud
Had stain'd its lucid face;
The mournful token of a shroud,
End of the humble and the proud,
The grave their resting-place.
And now to her the tale is told,
Her husband's hand and heart are cold:
And must she mourn the death of one
Whom she had loathed to look upon?
In customary garb array'd,
The pomp of grief must be display'd—
Dishevell'd tresses, streaming eyes,
The heart remaining in disguise—
She seem'd, distraction in her mien,
To feel her loss, if loss had been;
But all the burning tears she shed
Were for her own Majnún, and not the dead!

The rose that hail'd the purple morn,
All glistening with the balmy dew,
Look'd still more lonely when the thorn
Had been removed from where it grew.
But Arab laws had still their claim
Upon a virtuous widow's fame.
And what destroy'd all chance of blame?

Two years to droop behind the screen;
Two years unseeing, and unseen!
No, not a glance in all that time,
Blooming in life's luxurious prime,
Was e'er allow'd to womankind;
Since, but to household faces blind,
She must at home her vigils keep,
Her business still to groan and weep.
And Lailí weeps; but who can tell
What secrets may her bosom swell?
The beauteous eyes in tears may swim,
The heart may throb, but not for him
Who in the grave unconscious sleeps—
Alone for Majnún Lailí weeps!
Accustom'd hourly to rehearse
Her distant lover's glowing verse,
Framed like a spell to charm and bless,
And soothe her heart's extreme distress.

* * * *

"O what a night! a long and dreary night!
It is not night, but darkness without end;
Awful extinction of ethereal light,
Companionless I sit, without one friend.

Is the immortal source of light congeal'd?
Or has the dreadful day of judgment come?
Nature's fair form beneath a pall conceal'd;
Oh! what a night of soul-destroying gloom!

Can the shrill wakener of the morn be dead?
  Is the Mowazzin heedless of his trust?
Has the lone warder from his watch-tower fled,
  Or, weary of his task, return'd to dust?

O God! restore to me the joyous light
  Which first illumed my heart—the golden ray
Of youthful love—that from this prison, night,
  I may escape and feel the bliss of day!"

Years, days, how slowly roll they on!
And yet, how quickly life is gone!
The future soon becomes the past—
Ceaseless the course of time. At last
The morning came; the king of day
Arose in festival array,
And Lailí's night had pass'd away:
Her morn of beauty o'er her face,
Shining, resumed its wonted grace;
And with soft step of fairy lightness
She moved, a glittering moon in brightness.
And what was now her highest aim?
The impulse quivering through her frame?
Her secret love, so long conceal'd,
She now without a blush reveal'd,
And first she call'd her faithful Zӯd,
On many a tender mission tried,
In whom her heart could best confide:—

"To-day is not the day of hope,
Which only gives to fancy scope;
It is the day our hopes completing,
It is the lover's day of meeting!
Rise up! the world is full of joy;
Rise up! and serve thy mistress, boy;
Together, where the cypress grows,
Place the red tulip and the rose;
And let the long-dissever'd meet—
Two lovers, in communion sweet."

* * * *

They met; but how? hearts long to joy unknown
Know not what 'tis to be, except alone;
Feeling intense had check'd the power to speak;
Silent confusion sat upon each cheek;
Speechless with love unutterable, they
Stood gazing at each other all the day.
Thus, when a chamber holds no golden store,
No lock protects the ever-open door;
But when rich hoards of gold become a lure,
A lock is placed to keep that wealth secure;
So when the heart is full, the voice is bound—
For ready speech with grief is rarely found.
Lailí, with looks of love, was first who caught
The soft expression of her bursting thought:
"Alas!" she said, as over him she hung,
"What wond'rous grief is this that chains the tongue?

The bulbul, famed for his mellifluous note,
Without the rose can swell his tuneful throat,
And when in fragrant bowers the rose he sees,
He warbles sweeter still his ecstasies.
Thou art the bulbul of the bright parterre,
And I the rose—why not thy love declare?
Why, being absent, whilst unseen by thee,
Arose to heaven thy voice and minstrelsy?
And now, at length, when we are met, alone,
Thy love has vanish'd, and thy voice is gone!"

A gush of tears to Majnún gave relief:
Words came:—"The misery mine, and mine the grief;
The memory of those lips, so balmy sweet,
Bound up my tongue, which would their charms repeat.
When I, a falcon, through the woodlands flew,
The spotted partridge never met my view;
And now, when I'm unequal to the flight,
The long-sought beauteous bird has come in sight:
The substance thou, in angel charms array'd,
And what am I? I know not—but a shade;
Without thee nothing. Fancy would enthrone
Us both together, melted into one;
And thus, united to each other, we
Are equal—equal in our constancy:
Two bodies with one heart and spirit the same;
Two tapers with one pure celestial flame;
Of the same essence form'd, together join'd,
Two drops in one, each soul to each resign'd."

He paused, and, with ineffable delight,
Lailí gazed on his glowing countenance,
So long estranged and hidden from her sight.
Now throbs his heart at every fondling glance:
The fragrance of her ringlets which enwreath
Her smooth round neck, her jasmine-scented breath,
The sweet confession of her tremulous eyes,
The ardent love which time and chance defies,
The chin of dimpled sweetness, the soft cheek,
The open ruby lips prepared to speak,
Madden his finer feelings, and again
A sudden tempest rushes through his brain;
Furious he gazes round him for a while,
Then looks at Lailí with a ghastly smile;
Rends off his Jama-dress in frantic mood,
Starts, as with more than human force endued,
And, shouting, hurries to the desert plain,
Follow'd by all his savage vassal-train.

* * * * *

His love was chaste and pure as heaven:
But by excess to madness driven,
Visions of rapture fill'd his soul;
His thoughts sublime despised control;
A joy allied to joys above
Was mingled with his dreamy love:
O Majnún! lost, for ever gone;
The world is full of love, but none,

None ever bow'd at beauty's shrine
With such a sinless soul as thine.

* * * * *

In summer all is bright and gay;
In autumn verdure fades away,
The trees assume a sickly hue,
Unnourish'd by the fragrant dew;
The genial sap, through numerous rills,
From root and branch and leaf distils;
But, drying in the chilly air,
The groves become despoil'd and bare;
Sapless, the garden's flowery pride
The winds disperse on every side,
And all that sight and smell delighted
Is by the ruthless season blighted.
So Lailí's summer hours have pass'd;
And now she feels the autumnal blast;
Her bowers, her blooming bowers, assail'd,
The perfume of the rose exhaled,
Its wither'd leaves bestrew the ground,
And desolation reigns around:
For, from the moment she beheld
Her lover's mental state unveil'd,
Her heart no consolation knew,
Deprived of hope's refreshing dew.
Ere that o'erwhelming misery came,
Thoughts of new life upheld her frame:

Amidst her bitterest weeping and distress,
'Mid the dark broodings of her loneliness,
Though crush'd her feelings, and the man she loved
A wanderer of the forest, strangely moved,
Still was there hope, still was her mental gaze
Fix'd on the expected joys of after-days.
But now all hope had perish'd!—she had seen
The frenzied workings of that noble mien:
The fit delirious, the appalling start,
And grief and terror seized her trembling heart.
No tears she sheds, but pines away
  In deep entire despair;
The worm has seized its destined prey,
  The blight is on that face so fair,
And fearful symptoms of a swift decay
Come o'er her delicate frame, that in the strife
She almost sinks beneath the load of life.
Feeling the ebbing of the vital tide,
She calls her weeping mother to her side.
"Mother! my hour is come, thou need'st no longer
    chide;
For now no longer can my heart conceal
What once 'twas useless to reveal;
Yet, spite of thy affection, thou
Mayst blame my fatal passion now.
But I have in my rapture quaff'd
Poison in love's delicious draught;

And feel the agony which sears
The soul, and dries the source of tears.
O mother! mother! all I crave,
When I am pillowed in my grave,
Is that the anguish-stricken youth,
Whose wonderous constancy and truth
Blended our souls in one, may come
And weep upon his Lailí's tomb.
Forbid him not; but let him there
Pour forth the flood of his despair,
And no unhallow'd step intrude
Upon his sacred solitude.
For he to me, my life, my stay,
Was precious as the light of day.
Amazing was his love, sublime,
Which mock'd the wonted power of time;
And when thou seest him grovelling near,
Wildly lamenting o'er my bier,
Frown not, but kindly, soothingly relate
Whate'er thou know'st of my disastrous fate.
Say to that woe-worn wanderer,—'All is o'er;
Lailí, thy own sad friend, is now no more;
From this world's heavy chains for ever free,
To thee her heart was given—she died for thee!
With love so blended was her life, so true
That glowing love, no other joy she knew.
No worldly cares her thoughts had e'er oppress'd;
The love of thee alone disturb'd her rest;

And in that love her gentle spirit pass'd,
Breathing on thee her blessing to the last.'"

The mournful mother gazed upon her child,
Now voiceless—though her lips imploring smiled;
Saw the dread change, the sudden pause of breath—
Her beauty settled in the trance of death;
And, in the frenzy of her anguish, tore
Her hoary locks, the 'broider'd dress she wore;
Dissolved in tears, her wild and sorrowing cries
Brought down compassion from the weeping skies,
And so intense her grief, she shivering fell
Prostrate upon the corse, insensible,
And never, never rose again—the thread
Of life was broke—both, clasp'd together, dead!

* * * * *

O world! how treacherous thou art!
With angel-form and demon's heart;
A rosary of beads in hand,
And, covertly, a trenchant brand.
The rolling heavens with azure glow,
But storms o'erwhelm our hopes below;
The ship is toss'd upon the shore,
The wanderer meets his friends no more;
On flowery field, or boisterous wave,
Alike is found a yawning grave;
For formless, riding through the air,
Devouring death is everywhere;

Khosrú, and Kai-kobád, and Júm,
Have all descended to the tomb;
And who, composed of mortal clay,
The universal doom can stay?
For this, in vain, have youth and age
Ponder'd o'er learning's mystic page;
No human power can penetrate
The mysteries of all-ruling fate;
Frail life is but a moment's breath;
The world, alas! is full of death.

How many wept that fair one, gone so soon!
How many wept o'er that departed moon!—
How many mourn'd with broken hearts for her!
How many bathed with tears her sepulchre!
Round her pure dust assembled old and young,
And on the sod their fragrant offerings flung;
Hallow'd the spot where amorous youth and maid
In after-times their duteous homage paid.

Again it was the task of faithful Zŷd,
Through far-extending plain and forest wide,
To seek the man of many woes, and tell
The fate of her, alas! he loved so well.
Loved, doated on, until his mind, o'erwrought,
Was crush'd beneath intolerable thought.
—With bleeding heart he found his lone abode,
Watering with tears the path on which he rode,

And beating his sad breast, Majnún perceived
His friend approach, and ask'd him why he grieved;
What withering sorrow on his cheek had prey'd,
And why in melancholy black array'd.
"Alas!" he cried, "the hail has crush'd my bowers;
A sudden storm has blighted all my flowers;
The cypress-tree o'erthrown, the leaves are sear;
The moon has fallen from her lucid sphere;
Lailí is dead!" No sooner was the word
Utter'd, no sooner the dread tidings heard,
Than Majnún, sudden as the lightning's stroke
Sank on the ground, unconscious, with the shock,
And there lay motionless, as if his life
Had been extinguish'd in that mortal strife.
But, soon recovering, he prepared to rise,
Rewaken'd frenzy glaring in his eyes,
And, starting on his feet, a hollow groan
Burst from his heart. "Now, now, I *am* alone!
Why hast thou harrowing words like these express'd?
Why hast thou plunged a dagger in my breast?
Away! away!" The savage beasts around
In a wide circle couch'd upon the ground,
Wondering look'd on, whilst furiously he rent
His tattered garments, and his loud lament
Rang through the echoing forest. Now he threads
The mazes of the shadowy wood, which spreads
Perpetual gloom, and now emerges where
Nor bower nor grove obstructs the fiery air;

Climbs to the mountain's brow, o'er hill and plain
Urged quicker onwards by his burning brain,
Across the desert's arid boundary hies;
Zÿd, like his shadow, following where he flies;
And when the tomb of Lailí meets his view,
Prostrate he falls, the ground his tears bedew;
Rolling distraught, he spreads his arms to clasp
The sacred temple, writhing like an asp:
Despair and horror swell his ceaseless moan,
And still he clasps the monumental stone.
"Alas!" he cries—"No more shall I behold
That angel-face, that form of heavenly mould.
She was the rose I cherish'd—but a gust
Of blighting wind has laid her in the dust.
She was my favourite cypress, full of grace,
But death has snatch'd her from her biding-place.
The tyrant has deprived me of the flower
I planted in my own sequester'd bower;
The Basil sweet, the choicest ever seen,
Cruelly torn and scatter'd o'er the green.
O beauteous flower! nipp'd by the winter's cold,
Gone from a world thou never didst behold.
O bower of joy! with blossoms fresh and fair,
But doom'd, alas! no ripen'd fruit to bear.
Where shall I find thee now, in darkness shrouded!
Those eyes of liquid light for ever clouded!
Where those carnation lips, that musky mole
Upon thy cheek, that treasure of the soul!

Though hidden from my view those charms of thine,
Still do they bloom in this fond heart of mine;
Though far removed from all I held so dear,
Though all I loved on earth be buried here,
Remembrance to the past enchantment gives,
Memory, blest memory, in my heart still lives.
Yes! thou hast quitted this contentious life,
This scene of endless treachery and strife;
And I like thee shall soon my fetters burst,
And quench in draughts of heavenly love my thirst:
There, where angelic bliss can never cloy,
We soon shall meet in everlasting joy;
The taper of our souls, more clear and bright,
Will then be lustrous with immortal light!"

He ceased, and from the tomb to which he clung
Suddenly to a distance wildly sprung,
And, seated on his camel, took the way
Leading to where his father's mansion lay;
His troop of vassal-beasts, as usual, near,
With still unchanged devotion, front and rear;
Yet, all unconscious, reckless where he went;
The sport of passion, on no purpose bent,
He sped along, or stopp'd; the woods and plains
Resounding with his melancholy strains;
Such strains as from a broken spirit flow,
The wailings of unmitigable woe;
But the same frenzy which had fired his mind
Strangely to leave his Lailí's grave behind,

Now drove him back, and with augmented grief,
All sighs and tears, and hopeless of relief,
He flings himself upon the tomb again,
As if he there for ever would remain
Fatally mingled with the dust beneath,
The young, the pure, the beautiful in death.
Closely he strain'd the marble to his breast,
A thousand kisses eagerly impress'd,
And knock'd his forehead in such desperate mood,
The place around him was distain'd with blood.
Alone, unseen; his vassals keep remote
Curious intruders from that sacred spot;
Alone, with wasted form and sombre eyes,
Groaning in anguish he exhausted lies;
No more life's joys or miseries will he meet,
Nothing to rouse him from this last retreat;
Upon a sinking gravestone he is laid,
The gates already opening for the dead!
Selim, the generous, who had twice before
Sought his romantic refuge, to implore
The wanderer to renounce the life he led,
And shun the ruin bursting o'er his head,
Again explored the wilderness, again
Cross'd craggy rock, deep glen, and dusty plain,
To find his new abode. A month had pass'd
'Mid mountain wild, when, turning back, at last
He spied the wretched sufferer alone,
Stretch'd on the ground, his head upon a stone

Majnún, up-gazing, recognised his face,
And bade his growling followers give him place;
Then said,—"Why art thou here again, since thou
Left me in wrath? What are thy wishes now?
I am a wretch bow'd down with bitterest woe,
Doom'd the extremes of misery to know,
Whilst thou, in affluence born, in pleasure nursed,
Stranger to ills the direst and the worst,
Can never join, unless in mockery,
With one so lost to all the world as me!"
Selim replied:—"Fain would I change thy will,
And bear thee hence,—be thy companion still:
Wealth shall be thine, and peace and social joy,
And tranquil days, no sorrow to annoy;
And she for whom thy soul has yearn'd so long
May yet be gain'd, and none shall do thee wrong."
—Deeply he groan'd, and wept:—"No more, no more!
Speak not of her whose memory I adore;
She whom I loved, than life itself more dear,
My friend, my angel-bride, is buried here!
Dead!—but her spirit is now in heaven, whilst I
Live, and am dead with grief—yet do not die.
This is the fatal spot, my Lailí's tomb,—
This the lamented place of martyrdom.
Here lies my life's sole treasure, life's sole trust;
All that was bright in beauty gone to dust!"
Selim before him in amazement stood,
Stricken with anguish, weeping tears of blood;

And consolation blandly tried to give.
What consolation? Make his Lailí live?
His gentle words and looks were only found
To aggravate the agonising wound;
And weeks in fruitless sympathy had pass'd,
But, patient still, he linger'd to the last;
Then, with an anxious heart, of hope bereft,
The melancholy spot, reluctant, left.
The life of Majnún had received its blight;
His troubled day was closing fast in night.
Still weeping, bitter, bitter tears he shed,
As grovelling in the dust his hands he spread
In holy prayer. "O God! thy servant hear!
And in thy gracious mercy set him free
From the afflictions which oppress him here,
That, in the Prophet's name, he may return to Thee!"
Thus murmuring, on the tomb he laid his head,
And with a sigh his wearied spirit fled.

* * * * *

And he, too, has perform'd his pilgrimage.
And who, existing on this earthly stage,
But follows the same path? whate'er his claim
To virtue, honour,—worthy praise, or blame;
So will he answer at the judgment-throne,
Where secrets are unveil'd, and all things known;
Where felon-deeds of darkness meet the light,
And goodness wears its crown with glory bright.
Majnún, removed from this tumultuous scene,
Which had to him unceasing misery been,

At length slept on the couch his bride possess'd,
And, wakening, saw her mingled with the bless'd.
There still lay stretch'd his body many a day,
Protected by his faithful beasts of prey;
Whose presence fill'd with terror all around,
Who sought to know where Majnún might be found:
Listening they heard low murmurs on the breeze,
Now loud and mournful, like the hum of bees;
But still supposed him seated in his place,
Watch'd by those sentinels of the savage race.
—A year had pass'd, and still their watch they kept,
As if their sovereign was not dead, but slept;
Some had been call'd away, and some had died—
At last the mouldering relics were descried;
And when the truth had caught the breath of fame,
Assembled friends from every quarter came;
Weeping, they wash'd his bones, now silvery white,
With ceaseless tears perform'd the funeral rite,
And, opening the incumbent tablet wide,
Mournfully laid him by his Lailí's side.
One promise bound their faithful hearts—one bed
Of cold, cold earth united them when dead.
Sever'd in life, how cruel was their doom!
Ne'er to be join'd but in the silent tomb!

THE minstrel's legend-chronicle
Which on their woes delights to dwell,

Their matchless purity and faith,
And how their dust was mix'd in death,
Tells how the sorrow-stricken Zỹd
Saw, in a dream, the beauteous bride,
With Majnún seated side by side.
In meditation deep, one night,
The other world flush'd on his sight
With endless vistas of delight—
The world of spirits;—as he lay
Angels appear'd in bright array,
Circles of glory round them gleaming,
Their eyes with holy rapture beaming;
He saw the ever-verdant bowers,
With golden fruit and blooming flowers;
The bulbul heard, their sweets among,
Warbling his rich mellifluous song;
The ring-dove's murmuring, and the swell
Of melody from harp and shell:
He saw within a rosy glade,
Beneath a palm's extensive shade,
A throne, amazing to behold,
Studded with glittering gems and gold;
Celestial carpets near it spread
Close where a lucid streamlet stray'd;
Upon that throne, in blissful state,
The long-divided lovers sate,
Resplendent with seraphic light:—
They held a cap, with diamonds bright;

Their lips, by turns, with nectar wet,
In pure ambrosial kisses met;
Sometimes to each their thoughts revealing,
Each clasping each with tenderest feeling.
—The dreamer who this vision saw
Demanded, with becoming awe,
What sacred names the happy pair
In Irem-bowers were wont to bear.
A voice replied:—" That sparkling moon
Is Lailí still—her friend, Majnún;
Deprived in your frail world of bliss,
They reap their great reward in this!"
Zŷd, wakening from his wonderous dream,
Now dwelt upon the mystic theme,
And told to all how faithful love
Receives its recompense above.

O ye, who thoughtlessly repose
On what this flattering world bestows,
Reflect how transient is your stay!
How soon e'en sorrow fades away!
The pangs of grief the heart may wring
In life, but Heaven removes the sting;
The world to come makes bliss secure,—
The world to come, eternal, pure.
What other solace for the human soul,
But everlasting rest—virtue's unvarying goal!

SAKI! Nazámi's strain is sung;
The Persian poet's pearls are strung;
Then fill again the goblet high!
Thou wouldst not ask the reveller why?
Fill to the love that changes never!
Fill to the love that lives for ever!
That, purified by earthly woes,
At last with bliss seraphic glows.

NOTES.

Line 1. *Saki! thou know'st I worship wine.*

Saki—cup-bearer. The cup-bearer and his ruby wine stand in about the same relation in Persia's poetry, as the muse and "Castalia's stream" in the Greek. The cup-bearer is the great inspirer. Indeed, the Muses were the tutelar goddesses of festivals and banquets.

Line 42. *That wine, which to the fever'd lip,*
With anguish parch'd, when given to sip,
Imparts a rapturous smile, and throws
A veil o'er all distracting woes.

The Nepenthe of Homer.

Line 48. *And lifts the mind, now grown elate,*
To Jamshid's glory, Jamshid's state.

The story of Jamshid is finely told in the Shahnameh. He was one of the early rulers of Persia, a prince surrounded with peculiar splendour and magnificence: he was, however, suddenly precipitated from his throne, and put to a terrible death; his body being fastened between two planks, and divided with a saw. See the Shahnameh, abridged, in prose and verse, by the author of the present work.

Line 81. *Thence his attainments Kais assiduous drew.*

Kais was the original name of the lover, and afterwards called Majnún in consequence of the madness produced by his passion.

Line 94. *Her richly flowing locks were black as night,*
And Lailí she was call'd—that heart's delight.

Lailí, in Arabic, signifies night: the name, however, has been referred to her colour, and she is accused of possessing no beauty but in the eyes of her lover, being short in stature, and dark in complexion. A poet is said to have addressed her, saying, "Art *thou* the person for whom Kais lost his reason? I do not see that thou art so beautiful." "Silence!" she said, "*thou* art not Majnún," Another observed to Majnún, "Lailí is not surpassing in beauty; what occasions this adoration?" "Thou dost not see Lailí with my eyes!" was his brief reply. Laura and Eloisa, and other celebrated fair ones, have been equally robbed of their personal charms; indeed, Laura has been even stripped of her mortality. Gibbon speaks of her as a nymph so shadowy, that her very existence has been questioned, and adds, in a note, "The allegorical interpretation prevailed in the fifteenth century; but the wise commentators were not agreed whether they should understand, by Laura, religion or virtue, or the Blessed Virgin!" However, according to Nazámi and history, Lailí not only existed in reality, but was exquisitely beautiful.

Line 180. *Khosrú, without his throne or crown.*

Khosrú, a king of Persia—a royal surname.

Line 208 *And Lailí! Lailí! rang around,*
As if enamour'd of that magic sound.

Thus Shakspeare, in "Twelfth Night,"

Holla your name to the reverberate hills,
And make the babbling gossip of the air
Cry out, Olivia!

Line 232. *That mole which adds to every look*
A magic spell I cannot brook.

The mole is a prodigious beauty among Oriental writers. Thus Hafiz, "If that maid of Shiraz would accept my hand, I would give for the black mole on her cheek the cities of Samarkand and Bokara." Sir William Jones, in his fine Ode, has omitted the chief point in the stanza which contains the passage just cited. He says

"Sweet maid, if thou wouldst charm my sight,
And bid these arms thy neck enfold,
That rosy cheek, that lily hand,
Would give thy poet more delight
Than all Bokara's vaunted gold,
Than all the gems of Samarkand."

In these verses, however sweet they may be, the original sentiment is utterly lost.

Line 238. *As Káf's ice-summit, cold.*

Káaf, the Caucasus.

Line 247. *The Evil eye has struck my heart.*

The slavish superstition about conjuration, witchcraft, and enchantment, is universal in the East. In love affairs, charms are concocted to produce every imaginable effect,—attachment, scorn, jealousy, &c. A ridiculous case of the evil eye, in a less sentimental matter, occurred to one of my native servants the other day. He was proceeding in a boat from Barrackpore to Calcutta, and, anxious to get on quickly, though against the tide, he abused the boatman for not exerting himself sufficiently on the occasion. He appears to have been greatly excited, and on his arrival complained to me of an excruciating headache, declaring that he had been bewitched by a look from the boatman. He lost his appetite; fever came on, and he applied, as usual on such emergencies, to his saint, to get "the charm dissolved;" but to no purpose. He continued without taking food, and at length obtained leave to return to his home in a distant province. There was, however, enough of natural cause in the intense heat of the sun, and the excitement of violent passion, to occasion the symptoms complained of; but all his fellow-servants believed him to be the victim of an evil eye. Talismans and spells are innumerable in Arabia and Persia. There is the *Sulwan*, or water poured from a kind of shell, or upon earth taken from the grave of a dead man, which they drink to the health of a person, as a cure for love, or any severe affliction. *Atfet*, small beads, hung by women round their necks, as a charm to gain the affections of their lovers. *Akret*, a spherical amulet, worn by some women round their waists, to prevent pregnancy and by others to favour conception. *Aksit*, an amulet in form of a knot, which women wear to keep their husbands faithful. *Kerchara*, an ass's head placed upon a pole in a garden, &c., to guard it from fascination. In laughing at these fooleries, however, we must remember the first statute of James I., c. 12, against offenders "that consult, covenant with, entertain, employ, or reward any evil spirit, to any intent," or "that exercise any witchcraft, enchantment, charm, or sorcery, whereby any person shall be killed, destroyed, consumed, or lamed in his body, or any part thereof," which said statute was not repealed till the 9th of George II.!!!

Line 265. *He saw her fresh as morning's scented air—*
Himself exhausted by incessant care.

This sort of antithesis, or contrast of condition, is common among the Persian poets, and they dwell upon it with great pleasure, if we may judge from the extent to which they proceed whenever an opportunity presents itself. There are several instances of it in the course of this poem.

Line 461. *The holy Kâba where the Prophet pray'd,*
Where Zam-Zam's waters yield their saving aid.

The Kâba at Mecca is traditionally said to have been built by the patriarch Abraham: it is at least of very ancient date. Gibbon says, "The Greek historian Diodorus has remarked a famous temple, whose superior sanctity was revered by *all* the Arabians: the linen or silken veil, which is annually renewed by the Turkish emperor, was first offered by a pious king of the Homerites, who reigned 700 years before the time of Mahomet. A spacious portico incloses the quadrangle of the Câba, a square chapel, twenty-four cubits long, twenty-three broad, and twenty-seven high; a door and a window admit the light; the double roof is supported by three pillars of wood; a spout (now of gold) discharges the rain-water, and the well Zem-zem is protected by a dome from accidental pollution. The precincts of Mecca enjoyed the rights of sanctuary, and in the last month of each year the city and temple were crowded with a long train of pilgrims, who presented their vows and offerings in the house of God. The same rites which are now accomplished by the faithful Mussulman were invented and practised by the superstition of the idolaters. At an awful distance they cast away their garments; seven times, with hasty steps, they encircled the Câba, and kissed the black stone; seven times they visited and adored the adjacent mountains; seven times they threw stones into the valley of Mina; and the pilgrimage was achieved, as at the present hour, by a sacrifice of sheep and camels, and the burial of their hair and nails in the consecrated ground." Vol. ix. p. 245.

Line 744. *She droop'd like broken-winged bird.*

"Like a broken-winged bird" is a common epithet, expressive of misfortune and affliction.

Line 1100. *Whatever hero felt his ponderous gerz,*
Was crush'd, though stedfast as the Mount Elbêrz.

Gerz, a mace or club. Elbêrz is a celebrated mountain in Persia, and forms a favourite simile in the Shahnameh of Firdausi. The immovable firmness of his heroes is generally compared to the Mount Elbêrz.

Line 1195. *Near where Forát's bright stream rolls on, reclined.*

The river Euphrates. The scene is laid in the country surrounding Bagdad.

Line 1290. *His tale is told; some Diw or Ghoul*
Had palsied his intrepid soul.

"Diw—demon, giant, devil, ghost, hobgoblin. The diws, genii, or giants, in Eastern mythology, are a race of malignant beings. The ghoul is an imaginary sylvan demon, of different shapes and colours, supposed to devour men and animals. Anything which suddenly attacks and destroys a man, or robs him of his senses."—Richardson.

Line 1378. *Empurpled Dijla's rolling stream.*

The river Tigris.

Line 1387. *Quickly her sharp disdain the bridegroom feels,*
And from her scornful presence shrinks and reels.

The original makes Lailí rather Amazonian at this juncture, which is not quite in keeping with the gentleness of her character. It says, she struck him such a blow, that he fell down as if he were dead.

Line 1436. *Close, side by side, from morn till night,*
Kissing and dalliance their delight.

Báshad hema roz gosh der gosh. Literally, Every day, ear in ear.

Line 1458. *A dangerous friend, a fatal foe,*
Prime breeder of a world of woe.

Afati-jehán, the calamity of the world. A common epithet applied in anger to the fair sex. Something in the spirit of Otway:—

"Who lost Marc Antony the world? a woman.
Who was the cause of a long ten-years' war,
And laid at last old Troy in ashes? woman,
Destructive, damnable, deceitful woman!"

Line 1748. *Like Suliman, o'er all extends his reign.*

No name is more famous in the East than Solomon. Omnipotence is said to have placed under his obedience not only mankind, but animals. The birds were his constant attendants, screening him like a canopy from the inclemencies of the weather.

Line 1840. *The smiling presage of a prosperous day.*

Literally, On that day he rose up on the right-hand side; a sign that his fortune would be auspicious.

Line 1858. *Her ringlets twisted like the graceful Jim;*
Her shape an Alif, and her mouth a Mim.

To make this Persian conceit, of not unfrequent occurrence, understood, it may be enough to say the letter Jím of the Persian as well as Arabic alphabet, is formed something like the capital T of the German text; the Alif, like our number One in writing, and the Arabic letter Mím a small horizontal oval.

Line 1866. *My heart is desolate, my joys are fled.*

The original runs, *Ber jigeram nimak fikanda*, Salt is thrown upon my heart, expressive of anguish. It is amusing to observe that, in Spanish, salt is used very differently, and made to signify endearment,—thus: *Salero del alma!* Salt-cellar of my soul! *Es muy salada,* She is very salt—she is very endearing.

Line 1921. *Adoring the Creator, she began—*

This is the usual process in Oriental composition: and there is not a document ever written in Arabic or Persian but has the letter *Alif,* at least, placed at the top of the page, signifying there is but one God. The poets are especially scrupulous in pious exordiums to the Deity.

Line 1831. *Fountain of Khizer, sparkling in the shade*

Khizer is the name of a prophet, who, according to Oriental tradition, was vizier and general to an ancient king of Persia. They say that he discovered and drank of the fountain of life, and that, in consequence, he will not die till the last trumpet. He is by some confounded with the prophet Elias, and, which is somewhat singular, likewise with St. George of England, whom they call Khizer Elias, imagining that the same soul animated both by transmigration.

Line 1948. *Life's sweetest flow'rets, in their brightest bloom,*
Turn'd to the bitterness of fell Zikûm.

An infernal tree, mentioned in the Korân, the fruit of which is supposed to be the heads of devils.

Line 2175. *Fate look'd at last with favouring eye.*

Literally, The day on which her food was not infested with flies. A day free from misfortune or annoyance.

Line 2316. *Grief smiles upon me, and I smile on grief.*

Shakespeare has something like this personification of grief in King John, act iii. scene 4.

Constance. Grief fills the room up of my absent child,
Lies in his bed, walks up and down with me;
Puts on his pretty looks, repeats his words,
Remembers me of all his gracious parts,
Stuffs out his vacant garments with his form:
Then, have I reason to be fond of grief.

Line 2327. *The bulbul o'er thy roses joyous stoops.*

The bulbul is the nightingale. The reader need scarcely be reminded of the fabled loves of the nightingale and the rose.

Line 2381. *And many a farsang he had rode.*

A parasang, a league.